WORKING THE LAND

Charlie Pye-Smith
and
Richard North

TEMPLE SMITH
LONDON

First published in Great Britain in 1984 by
Maurice Temple Smith Limited
Jubilee House, Chapel Road,
Hounslow, Middlesex, TW3 1TX

Pye-Smith, Charlie
 Working the land.
  1. Agriculture—Economic aspects—Great Britain
  —Case studies
  I. Title   II. North, Richard
  338.1'0722   HD1925

ISBN 0 85117 249 0

Typeset in 11pt on 12pt Plantin by
Tellgate Ltd., Dorset
Printed and bound in Great Britain at
The Camelot Press Ltd, Southampton

Contents

Acknowledgements

We are particularly indebted to the many farmers who shared both their knowledge and their time with us. We chose the busiest time in the farming calendar to tour the country but we received great kindness wherever we went. Our thanks go to Michael Chandler of Dorset, Stewart Crocker of Kent, Nicholas Horton-Fawkes of Yorkshire, Mrs Angela Hughes of Dorset, Mike Keeble of Yorkshire, Pete and Debbie King of Warwickshire, Michael Smith of Hampshire and Barry Wookey of Wiltshire.

Ralph Cobham and Russel Matthews of Cobham Resource Consultants kindly let one of us go on two farm tours which were part of their work for the Countryside Commission's Demonstration Farm Project. Our thanks go to both them and the two farmers, John Tabor of Essex and Poul Christensen of Oxfordshire.

Norman Weiss generously escorted one of us round his forest estate in the Chilterns and Eric Carter gave up some of his time to discuss the Farming and Wildlife Advisory Group's work. Peter Roberts of Compassion in World Farming, Melanie Roots his former colleague, and Dr Alan Long, advisor to the Vegetarian Society, discussed with us at great length the problems of animal welfare on the farm today. Professor Gerald Wibberley shared some of his considerable knowledge of the farming industry with us and Dr Mike Wilkinson, director of The Society for the Responsible Use of Resources in Agriculture and on the Land (RURAL), did likewise. He also suggested farmers we should visit, many of whom we did. Sue Clifford and Angela King discussed with us the problems of conservation on British farms. David Stickland of Organic Farmers & Growers Ltd proved an invaluable source of knowledge and information on organic farming. To all these people we offer our sincere thanks. Without their help *Working the Land* would have been a thinner and a poorer book. Needless to say whatever mistakes or errors of judgement are found in these pages are solely our responsibility.

Finally, we must thank Epson Corporation. The Epson HX-20 Portable Computer which they lent us to write *Working the Land* made our task infinitely easier and more enjoyable.

Note

We have for the most part used the old Imperial units of size and weight, writing of acres and pounds rather than hectares and kilograms, since the old system is still more familiar to most people. The exception to this is that where we are quoting technical figures of the kind that are now normally given in metric units we have used the metric system. We have also used the metric tonne throughout, since it is so close to the Imperial ton. The following conversions may be useful:

1 hectare – 2.471 acres
1 metre – 1.094 yards
1 kilogram – 2.2 pounds
1 tonne – 1.016 tons

I have embraced industrialism . . . all because I want to be through with it, want to get to the other side of it, into a world of electrical power and mechanical plenty when man can once more return to the land, not as a peasant but as a lord. The ether will deliver us the power that the old landlords extracted from the serfs: there will be no need to enslave a single human soul. But we shall be in contact with the land; we shall have soil and not cement under our feet; we shall live from the produce of our fields and not from the canned pulp of our factories.

Herbert Read

1 *The Measure of the Problem*

'We've got the length of this Parliament to pull ourselves together,' says Michael Chandler. 'I don't think that's going to be enough time. . . . We may well end up having a lot of controls we don't want.'

Chandler pushes through the thick undergrowth beside the River Frome, a dazzlingly clear Dorset chalk stream which runs through the seven hundred acres of his tenanted farm just a short walk south of Tolpuddle, village of the famous martyrs. He is a big man with a genial smile, a model farmer and passionate conservationist. He periodically stoops to observe the insect life. He points out the brilliant blue-banded agrions – damsel flies which dart between the reeds – and butterflies like comma and tortoiseshell.

When he took over the tenancy on Hurst Farm at the end of the war Chandler carved many of the pastures and arable fields which sustain him and his dairy herd today from scrub and woodland; but he left twelve acres along the riverside and saved some wet meadowland. Today he is doing what many leaders of the agricultural industry claim to be impossible without generous government support: he is farming his land profitably and providing substantial havens for wildlife.

Chandler is the sort of farmer that townspeople dream about. He's also the sort of farmer that the National Farmers' Union (NFU) and the Country Landowners' Association (CLA) – the heavyweights of rural politics – claim presides over our much-beleaguered countryside: the custodian who looks after the landscape for the rest of us. As we stood next to the Frome on that July morning in 1983, with warblers singing in the reeds, trout rising to pluck flies off the water surface and a gentle breeze ruffling the willows, the woes of the agricultural industry seemed a long way off. But such is the power of the conservation lobby, and such is popular concern about the fate

1

of our wildlife and landscape, that any government other than that presently in power is likely to introduce controls which will severely restrict what the farmer can do. Unless the farmers 'pull themselves together' they will soon find themselves having to apply for permission before they pull out a hedgerow or plough up an old pasture. The irresponsible ones who are wrecking the countryside are few, comparatively speaking, but the damage they do is out of all proportion – tearing down woodlands which for centuries have provided solace and inspiration to many, draining marshes which for generations have supported snipe, redshank and orchid, ploughing up meadows whose present flora is directly descended from plants which were grazed by the sheep of the seventeenth century. It is the inability of today's farmers to censure this handful of wreckers which has led to the spectre of draconian legislation.

Chandler is the chairman of the Dorset branch of the Farming and Wildlife Advisory Group. The FWAG, both in counties like Dorset and nationally under the adept leadership of an ex-Ministry-of-Agriculture man, Eric Carter, is becoming increasingly influential. Whether it can help to save the farmers from the legislators remains to be seen.

While we stood surveying the River Frome and wondering if the otters would ever return, the first fields of winter wheat were going under the combine. And the first smoke signals of the annual harvest trouble were rising off the Wiltshire plains to the north. Straw burning may be one of the most visible aspects of waste on the farm today but it is by no means the only one.

Since the last war the farm has become a very different place from that which saw the hen, the pig, the cow and the sheep all living together on the same plot of land, along with the rotating crops of wheat, barley, mangle worzels, cow cabbage and turnip. The trend has been towards increasing specialisation, with arable crops concentrated in the east – particularly in the belt of flat land which stretches from the capital up to the Vale of York – and with dairying and beef rearing concentrated in the wetter west and on the hills. Such over-specialisation has led to massive waste of straw – an estimated 6 million tonnes went up in smoke in the autumn of 1983. The autumn, as far as the public is concerned, should be the 'season of mists and mellow fruitfulness' and whatever the pros and cons of straw and stubble burning (we discuss them in Chapter 4) this year's

2

catalogue of burning disasters led to calls for a ban on an unprecedented scale.

British oil and gas, and consequently nitrogenous fertilizers, are soon going to run short and become so expensive that the farmer must look for alternatives. The alternative comes out of the backsides of cattle, sheep and pigs. The problem is going to be getting them back onto the farm. The specialist arable man has been living in a fool's paradise, with Common Market subsidies retaining artificially high prices for his product and any number of financial inducements helping him not only to keep his head above water but, in many cases, to make very handsome profits.

Working the Land is inevitably going to be gloomy in places: the rural crisis is of deep concern to all people in this country. But our gloom is tempered by optimism. This book is as much a story about the men and women who are already farming as though the twenty-first century, with all its constraints, is just around the corner, as it is about the intense cruelty of certain farming practices, about the dreadful waste (of straw, of muck, of energy), about the massive and profligate channelling of public funds from the Treasury and the coffers of Brussels, about the destruction of wildlife and landscape, and about the poor state of the nation's health.

This book is not anti-farmer; rather, it is a celebration of the ways in which land could, should, and soon must be used. Nobody ever again wants to see the sort of rural depressions that bedevilled this country in the latter decades of the last century and the years between the two great wars. 'During my boyhood,' recalls Professor Gerald Wibberley, the agricultural economist who was raised between the wars on the infertile hills where Herefordshire borders Wales, 'the countryside was shaggy and unkempt. And so were we. We were also hungry.' There is a strong feeling of remembrance according to Wibberley, a remembrance among farmers of that time when nobody cared about them until the war came and once again the urban population relied not on cheap imports from the Empire but on the produce of Britain's own soils.

Since the last war successive governments have ensured – through all sorts of funding and market manipulation – that the depressions of the past have not fallen again upon the countryside. But as this book shows, agricultural support – an

3

annual £3 billion of it – has not benefited everyone in the countryside: many small farmers have suffered. Furthermore the sums of money dispensed by our own Ministry of Agriculture, Fisheries and Food (MAFF) and by the EEC's Common Agricultural Policy (CAP) have become so great that the EEC is threatened with bankruptcy, and the taxpayer and consumer who foot the bill are at last saying 'enough is enough'.

Whilst the larks spiralled up above the Frome and smoke blackened the skies to the north grim news was drifting across the Channel from Brussels. Farm spending for 1983 was running at about 40 per cent over the estimate: to the annual budget of £9000 millions the Commission had to add another £1090 million just to prevent the CAP from collapsing. As we write the harvests are in, the September skies are clear again and the Council of Ministers is haggling over CAP reforms. So severe is the overspending crisis that by 1984 we may witness the disintegration of the CAP, Europe's only common policy.

Unravelling the complexities of the Common Agricultural Policy can be a nightmare (and it is one which we can postpone for a while) but it is worth briefly indicating where this money – our money – goes. Take the estimated figures for Community farm spending in 1983. Of the £8590m which came from EEC coffers £2510m will have gone to subsidize milk production and £1340m to cereal production. (The UK share forecast for market regulation for 1982/83 was £321 million for milk and £374 million for cereals.) There is a very simple reason for this massive EEC spending on milk and cereals: we produce too much of them and the taxpayer has to pay to help store the surpluses and to subsidize their sales onto the world market.

Support for the farming industry before we joined the EEC was justified by the need for this country to become self-sufficient in temperate food products. But as Professor Wibberley points out, 'we are in an absolutely new situation. We are much nearer self-sufficiency and the new problem is overproduction. We are embarrassed by domestic surpluses and we've adopted a very narrow dumping policy.' For the first time in her history Britain became a net exporter of wheat in 1983, an astonishing achievement for a country whose main crop is grass, and despite self-sufficiency in milk and gross overproduction of many milk derivatives, output has continued to rise, and indeed has been encouraged to rise by CAP policies.

The Community now overproduces sugar, poultrymeat, barley, wheat, butter, skimmed milk powder and cheese and is self-sufficient in oats, potatoes, eggs, fresh milk products, beef and veal, pigmeat and fresh vegetables.[1]

It is time – and the farmers admit this – to call a halt to excessive production. Not only is it costly to the taxpayer and consumer, it represents a futile waste of many resources. And far from making us self-reliant in times of crisis, it makes us terribly vulnerable. In August 1983 Sir Herman Bondi, former chief scientific advisor to the Ministries of Defence and of Energy, Dr John Bowman, former director of the Centre for Agricultural Strategy, and Jonathon Bates wrote in *The Times*:

> There are three critically essential inputs to the modern agricultural system: fossil fuels, electricity and water. A disruption to the availability of any, even for a few days, would have serious consequences. There are just not enough people available to milk cows by hand. Equally, if the electricity fails there will be no way to save the bulk of the milk produced. In the absence of water and ventilation, poultry in battery cages and broiler houses would have to be killed. Without fossil fuels it would become extremely difficult to distribute food.

Even if we ignore the nuclear dimension, the three experts suggest, attacks on power stations, fertilizer factories and so on will completely disrupt our agricultural system, 'reducing production by perhaps four-fifths'. Thus one of the main arguments used to justify the relentless push towards self-sufficiency, and therefore to justify high levels of state and Community support, is a perverse sham. Today's highly mechanised farming systems and food distribution patterns make mass starvation more likely in a future war rather than the opposite.

'The problem with farming today,' said a Welsh shepherd at the '83 Royal Show, 'is that there's no real market. We've been living in cloud cuckoo land. We've forgotten that our survival is ultimately going to depend on the public buying our food. The day may come when they say "Enough is enough: we'll buy our

---

[1] At points signalled by these references, there is a note in the section of Additional Information at the end of the book.

sheep elsewhere if you don't mind." ' He added with a grin that he hoped the sheepmeat regime carried on. 'I'm doing very nicely for a change.'

'One day,' wrote Oliver Walston, a big arable man, in *Farmers Weekly* in 1983, 'the tax-paying public is going to wake up with a start and decide that it is fed up with the Common Agricultural Policy. Until this actually happens, of course, I shall continue accepting subsidies with alacrity and gratitude.'

Well, that day has very nearly arrived. The public will not stand for the CAP much longer, certainly not in its present form, nor will it stand for giving agriculture the support to which it has become used. Farmers will have to help themselves and if the industry is seen to be relying on its own ingenuity, then, if it does have to come to the tax-payer and the consumer for help in the next century, it will be much more likely to get it.

Barry Wookey (whom we shall meet in Chapter 5) is one man who is helping himself. He farms 1700 acres of downland in Wiltshire, and he has foreseen the shortages of the future and reacted to the serious damage he believes chemical farming is causing, by going organic. Over the last ten years he has weaned his fields off chemical fertilizers and pesticides (like junkies, they take time to adapt to the health kick) and he is producing over 2 tonnes of hard, bread-making wheat per acre. Financially Wookey is doing as well as the average chemical farmer. His yields are slightly lower, but so are his inputs. At a time of energy scarcity and surplus production it is the low-input farmer who is the least drain on resources, both environmental and financial.

The controversy over low inputs and high inputs is central to this book. To take one example, milk yields have increased over the last decade from an average of 4,000 litres per cow per year to 5,000 litres. This dramatic increase, however, can be attributed almost entirely to concentrate feeding rather than to better production of grass or more efficient use of it. Drugs and hormones have also done much to boost the output of livestock. There are farmers, however, who show that decent yields can be achieved without heavy concentrate feeding and massive doses of nitrogen on the supporting grasslands. On his Yorkshire estate, perched on the slopes to the north of Otley, Nicholas Horton-Fawkes runs a herd of Ayreshires. By rotating his crops in the old fashioned way, by utilizing every ounce of waste – what goes into the cow's mouth owes much of its bulk to what left at the rear end in the months before – and by careful management of his grazing lands, Horton-Fawkes runs a highly successful low-input enterprise. He uses much less concentrate feed than the average dairy farmer yet his cows produce over 5,500 litres of milk per year.

There is a well-known farming adage that one should live as though one were going to die tomorrow but farm as though one were going to live forever. It is this philosophy which has been forsaken since the last war, in the frenzied rush to make our farmland and animals produce more and more. While the soils have been switched from a natural diet of muck and benign pesticides onto a chemical menu, our farm stock has suffered from intensive production methods which have probably disturbed and outraged the eating, and largely urban, public even more than the production of surpluses. In the chapter on Animal Factory we investigate the fate of the hen, a creature not blessed with great intelligence but one which doesn't deserve the terrible cruelty of the modern battery system. Over 96 per cent of the eggs laid in this country come from the battery system, although one wouldn't think so by looking at the remarkably misleading ways in which the product is advertised. It is only a matter of time before the battery system is banned (the House of Commons' Select Committee on Agriculture called for a ban in 1981) and in Chapter 3 we go down to a farm in Hampshire where two adventurous brothers have shown that the free-range system is not only humane but makes money.

At the Royal Agricultural Show at Stoneleigh in 1983 a vet from the Ministry's Agricultural Development and Advisory Service (ADAS) accompanied one of us round the pig unit. 'We can't call this farming, can we?' he said, as we peered into the dim ultra-violet gloom of an intensive pig unit. 'Look at the way those ones are behaving.' He pointed to a couple in one corner. One pig was gnawing in a frenzied, demonic way at the bolt of the door which lay between it and freedom. Meanwhile its tail was being chewed by another pig.

Nearly a decade ago an editorial in the *British Medical Journal* suggested that 'A start could and should be made towards integrating nutrition and food policies in Britain. Furthermore sensible and regular nutritional advice should be incorporated in the Common Agricultural Policy of the EEC.' Sadly, the advice of the medical experts has been consistently ignored. *Working the Land* will show that our future agricultural policies, whether they relate to the amount of dairy products that we produce, the quality of our cereals or the processing of our food, must be formulated in the context of today's overburdened hearts, sagging stomachs, irritable bowels and intestinal cancers. In the same magazine one doctor, Richard Mackarness of Basingstoke District Hospital, wrote that 'Any mother whose child's intractable eczema has cleared with the elimination of cow's milk would agree that this dairy product should carry the same Government health warning as cigarettes.'

Working the Land is as much about people as it is about the soil, the farm animal and the market place. Each of us, tracing our roots back through the family tree, needs only go back a few generations to find that they sprang from the soil of our fields rather than the concrete and cobbles of the towns. Most of us are ignorant of the ways in which the countryside is managed yet most, despite this ignorance, hold it in great affection, an affection which one suspects owes much to our common origin in a peasant society. At the beginning of the nineteenth century, well after the Industrial Revolution was going at full steam, over a third of the British labour force worked on the land. By 1850 this figure had dropped to a fifth and by 1900 to a tenth. Today agriculture provides employment for around 700,000 people.

Government and EEC policies tend to view the farm worker as just another variable in the equation which links inputs and outputs, a variable which must be dispensed with as far as possible in the name of efficiency. The following exchange was reported to have taken place between two agricultural ministers, Peter Walker of Britain and Josef Ertl of Germany (both have moved to new pastures now). It is highly revealing of the attitude which pervades Ministry of Agriculture policy and Britain's interpretation of EEC policy.

Peter Walker: 'They are not real farmers in your dairy industry. They are chaps working on the production line in your motor industry with five cows at home to look after in the evening.'

Josef Ertl: 'You are quite right. Perhaps that is the reason why Volkswagon does so much better than British Leyland. Perhaps if you gave all those British Leyland workers five cows things would be rather better for it.'

As it happens we shall not be advocating any great shift of the dairy industry into the backyards of Cowley or Longbridge. What we shall do is show how there are farmers today who are going out of their way to employ more people on their land, rather than less.

While the labour force has continued to decline, farm size has continued to increase. All the fiscal policies operating in the countryside favour farm amalgamation and the trend away from tenanted land to owner-occupation.[2] And while the size of farm holdings continues to increase, with over three-quarters of all land sold in the 1970s being bought by those who already owned land, the opportunities for young men and women to find tenancies have decreased. One of the only ways in which farm workers who lack the capital to buy land have been able to get into farming has been through the county council tenancy system. This is now under attack by the government, which is encouraging councils to sell off their small holdings.

One of the consequences of post-war agricultural policies has been the decline of rural services and communities. To the daytripper from Leeds, the Yorkshire Dales, with their solid villages of limestone houses and patchwork of grazing meadows hemmed in between stone walls, may appear very much as they were a century ago. But appearances are deceptive. East Witton, a village in mid-Wensleydale, lies halfway up the fell which stretches from the rushing waters of the Ure to the heather moors to the west. It is a small village, consisting mainly of two rows of stone cottages, a fine green which divides the two rows, a small chapel and a squat church. In 1890 the 2,609 acres which comprised East Witton Township Within were home to 240 inhabitants. Among these were two gamekeepers, two blacksmiths, a cartwright, three cowkeepers, two shoemakers, one of whom doubled as the sexton, a schoolmaster who was also parish clerk, two shopkeepers, a butcher, a stonemason, a tailor, an architect, a seedsman, and a joiner and builder. The Reverend Wilkie looked after the faithful while William Metcalf and Mrs Elizabeth Towler catered for the thirsty in the Blue Lion and the Forester's Arms. There were ten farmers and Miss Dinsdale ran the post office. Outwardly the village has changed little over the last hundred years. But today there are no trades practised in Witton. A farmer runs a combined butchers, post office and grocery, and one pub caters for a tiny trade. There are only a handful of people who live in the village

9

and work locally and the largest proportion of the village consists of retired people. Second homes abound. East Witton is no freak example; what has happened here has happened throughout the country.

But the trend can be reversed, and that is exactly what many of the farmers we visited are doing. Down on the Kent Weald Neil Wates has increased his staff from 7 to 22 since 1976. He foresees the inevitable curbs on milk production, so he has decided to add value to milk before it reaches the farm gate. He's going to make cheese. At the same time his farm converts slurry into energy. At the moment the economics don't favour it, but as energy prices inevitably continue to rise, they soon will do.

'We may end up having a lot of controls we don't want,' said Michael Chandler, the farmer we quoted at the beginning of this chapter. In this book we have advocated very few, believing that voluntary progress is better. 'Throughout the world,' says Professor Wibberley, 'peasants have always been outwitting governments.' That is an admirable talent; but for the sake of both the farmer and everyone else, let us hope that the reforms we need can be brought about by the farmers themselves rather than through bureaucratic repression. There will then be no need to outwit government.

2 Food Fit for People

At the end of the last century Rider Haggard, better known as the author of *King Solomon's Mines* than as a Norfolk farmer, set off on a tour of rural England. He tells the story of an old Essex farm labourer whom he met, a man called John Lapwood. For months at a time Lapwood lived on bread and onions. 'These onions he ate until they took the skin off the roof of his mouth, blistering it to whiteness. . . . They had no tea, but his wife imitated the appearance of that beverage by soaking a burnt crust of bread in boiling water. On this diet he became so feeble that the reek of the muck which it was his duty to turn made him sick and faint.' Haggard exhorted the reader of his *Rural England* to think of the labourer 'with his nine shillings a week, and ten souls to feed, house and clothe, while bread stood at a shilling a loaf'.

During the closing years of the last century the working class in Britain spent 71 per cent of their earnings on food and drink while the middle classes spent slightly less than half. Today we spend on average 21 per cent of our earnings on food and drink, and the disparity between rich and poor has narrowed to the extent that very few Britons suffer from malnutrition, except by over-eating. Nevertheless wealth still exerts an important dietary influence. The poor, according to John Burnett's classic social history of diet, *Plenty and Want*, eat 56 per cent less fruit than the rich, 31 per cent less fresh meat, 28 per cent less cheese, 26 per cent less milk and 19 per cent less fresh green vegetables. However, they consume 57 per cent more potatoes, 33 per cent more cereal products and 32 per cent more sugar. The poor tend to eat more white bread and more fatty mince (for example, in sausages) and suffer more from coronary heart disease. They also tend to smoke more and breast feed less than the more affluent.

Post-war agricultural policies have taken all sorts of factors into account but never the national diet. This is a remarkable

11

omission and one which is leading to a furore in medical circles. Overeating and poor eating habits have become killers on a frightening scale. The high rates of coronary heart disease, diabetes, diverticular disease, gall bladder disease, constipation and bowel cancer in the western world are closely related to our diet, which is rich in fats, sugar and salt but low in fibre.

In July 1983 the *Sunday Times* got its hands on a document which was to become known as the James Report, a document which highlighted the disturbing trends in our diet and advocated shifts in our eating habits which, if eventually followed, would have dramatic effects on both the farming and the food processing industries.

In 1979 the government set up a committee to report on the state of the British diet and to recommend improvements. The committee – the National Advisory Committee on Nutrition Education (NACNE) – consisted of doctors, nutritionists and other experts. In 1981 the committee reported – and its report was promptly suppressed by the Department of Health and Social Security. The findings of the report were very much in line with previous medical thinking, though Professor James's team went further than most by putting figures to the dietary changes which were desirable. Despite strong opposition, the team pressed ahead and produced another report in late 1982, and a further draft in April 1983. Such is the importance of this document that we must summarise its findings and recommendations at some length.

The report states that 'the consensus of medical opinion is that the population should not be consuming the type of diet currently eaten in Britain.' No less than 39 per cent of all men and 32 per cent of all women are overweight, the main culprits being fats and sugars. 'Death rates for coronary heart disease in the UK are among the highest in the world,' and the report says that much of it could be prevented by a reduction of fat in the diet from 40 per cent to 30-35 per cent of our total energy intake.

The report links the following list of diseases with excessive consumption of fats, sugars and salt, or inadequate consumption of fibre: cancer of the large bowel and colon, diverticular disease and irritable bowels – too little fibre; diabetes and gall bladder disease – too much fat and sugar and too little fibre; heart disease – too much fat; strokes – too much fat and salt. It has been conservatively estimated that diet-related diseases cost the National Health Service around £1000 million a year.

The James Report recommends the following changes in the national diet over the next five years. The intake of fat should be cut by 10 per cent, primarily by reducing the amount of dairy produce and meat we consume. Our sugar consumption should be cut by 10 per cent. And we should cut our salt intake by 8 per cent. The report recommends a 25 per cent increase in fibre intake, most of which would come from increasing our consumption of bread (of the wholemeal, not cotton wool variety), potatoes, fresh fruit and fresh vegetables. Many nutritionists envisage more dramatic dietary changes over a longer period. Over fifteen years we should aim to halve sugar consumption (we could then be self-sufficient in this crop) and reduce fat consumption by 25 per cent.

The suppression of the James Report infuriated the medical profession. The magazine *Lancet* suggested that the food industry 'apparently disliked much of what it read and seems to have got the Department of Health to suppress or at any rate delay the report. If so the department should think again, quickly.' And the quicker the better if the number of people dying of heart disease is to be reduced from the annual 174,000, if the stroke count is to be reduced from 78,000, and if the 11,000 people dying every year of bowel and colon cancers are to be saved.

Milk: time to kill the sacred cow

The dairy industry will be one of the hardest hit by any reduction in consumption of animal fats. Dairy fats provide more than a third of the total fat intake according to Ministry of Agriculture figures. A study carried out at Reading University's Centre for Agricultural Strategy in 1978 (*Food, Health and Farming: Reports of panels on the implications for UK agriculture*, ed. C.J. Robbins) found that 'the average UK diet contains approximately twice the amount of protein that is required, and deficiencies of fat soluble vitamins are rare and can be prevented in ways other than the consumption of large amounts of fat.' (Milk and cheese provide about a quarter of dietary protein while butter and cream are sources of fat soluble vitamins.) The report suggested that the reduction of the fat content of milk from 3·8 per cent to 2·0 per cent might be more acceptable than the reduction of milk consumption itself (although there will be the problem of getting rid of the butterfat from skimming). Such a measure would reduce fat consumption by 7 per cent. The James Report points out that milk fat is mostly saturated fat (one of the main culprits in fat-related diseases) and says that 'The policy of promoting milk consumption would be more readily compatible with a planned reduction in fat intake if fresh milk with a low fat content were readily available for doorstep delivery.' In fact, both the Reading and James Reports are being most obliging to the milk industry by suggesting that fat content rather than just consumption should be reduced.

While the public were mulling over the findings of the James Report, the European Commission was drawing up proposals to deal with Europe's dairy surpluses which would be directly contrary to all that the doctors were advocating. By 1981 the EEC was 101 per cent self sufficient in fresh milk products, and self sufficient in cheese, butter, concentrated milk and skimmed milk powder to the tune of 105 per cent, 119 per cent, 148 per cent and 343 per cent respectively. In Britain in 1983 there were 3·33 million dairy cows, producing much more than we needed. Despite the fact that liquid consumption had fallen from 7,433 million litres at the beginning of the seventies to 7,305 by the end, total sales rose spectacularly by over 16 per cent, the increase being taken up by the manufacturing industry. Consequently cheese and butter production has shot up, and overproduction has been encouraged by EEC policy.[1] Despite all the problems of storing and getting rid of surpluses (the total CAP cost for dairying including market regulation, storage of surpluses and so on was over £2·5 billion in 1983), milk producers in Britain shared a record £2 billion payout in the year ending 31 March 1983 according to the Milk Marketing Board. The MMB, rather than accepting that production curbs were necessary, argued in favour of proposals which would improve the market for milk and dairy products.

So what was the Commission's reaction to the crippling over-spending on the dairy sector? It put forward proposals that would raise the fat content of all types of milk. The reason: to take the tip off the butter mountain which by autumn 1983 stood at 800,000 tonnes in Europe and 93,000 tonnes in Britain. The Commission was also considering other ways of getting rid of the butter besides adding it to the slimmers' skimmed and semi-skimmed milks. It was contemplating selling it cheap to food manufacturers. (Pastry and icecream makers already get butter at between a third and a half of the market price of £2100 a tonne and the Commission was considering extending such generosity to the manufacturers of biscuits, cakes and sweets, three classes of food which the doctors suggest we should consume in smaller quantities.) Furthermore the Commission wanted butter to replace the much safer unsaturated vegetable oils in these industries. All these measures have an air of desperation: milk production continues to expand (by 5 per cent in the UK in 1982) and the butter subsidy for consumers (14p a pound in Britain) has not led to increased consumption. So while the doctors advocate decreasing the fat content of milk from 3·5 per cent to 2·0 per cent the Commission is arguing in favour of increasing it by 0·2 per cent.

According to MAFF figures for 1976, dairy products contributed 36·2 per cent of dietary fat, of which 14·2 per cent was from milk, 4·5 per cent from cheese and 16·3 per cent from butter. The Reading group thought that educational rather than legislative action was needed to reduce fat consumption in cheese. This could be done by promoting lower fat cheeses. Some, like Stilton and Cheddar, are very high in fat (40 and 35 per cent respectively) while Camembert and Edam are very low in fat (both around 22 per cent). Butter, however, does not deserve any dispensation as it weighs in with an 85 per cent fat content. Butter consumption has been on the decline for a long time and the decline is expected to continue. The Reading group claimed that there was no justification in nutritional terms for subsidizing it, and hinted that a tax might be more appropriate. (In the United States, incidentally, the average person eats only 27 per cent of the butter we eat in this country.)

'The British government,' says Professor Haines of the Department of Agricultural Economics at the University College of Wales, Aberystwyth, 'has simultaneously deplored the milk surplus and continued to pay grants to improve or expand dairy units.' This is no longer excusable. The only proper way to reduce the embarrassment of surpluses is to reduce production.

A leaner future

One of the sons of East Witton, the Wensleydale village we referred to in the first chapter, was George Neville, who became an Archbishop of York. When he was consecrated he laid on a feast for the nobility, gentry and clergy, the like of which we would never see now some five centuries later. This is what his guests ate: 75 cwt of wheat, 71,300 gallons of ale, 26,000 gallons of wine, 105 gallons of spiced wine, 400 bucks, does and roebucks, 80 fat oxen, 6 wild bulls, 1,000 wethers, 300 calves, 200 kids, 300 hogs, 300 pigs, 4,000 rabbits, 3,000 capons, 100 peacocks, 200 cranes, 3,000 geese, 2,000 chickens, 4,000 pigeons, 200 bitterns, 4,000 ducks, 4,000 young herons, 200 pheasants, 500 partridges, 4,000 woodcock, 400 plovers, 100 curlews, 100 quails, 1,000 egrets, 1,506 hot venison pasties, 4,000 of the same cold, 300 pike, 300 bream, 8 seals and 4 porpoises. We don't know how many people ate this meal but there were 62 cooks, 515 kitcheners and 1,000 servers.

Some of the meats eaten by the archbishop and his guests we can obtain today. Others we can't. Curlews, plovers, herons, seals and porpoises are protected species. Cranes and egrets have become extinct in this country. The rest we can buy, except perhaps wild bulls.

The medieval diners knew nothing about saturated fats and not a lot about coronary heart disease. For most, meat was a luxury; and it was not so fatty. The fat and lean composition of different wild and domestic species varies considerably. The pig is 38 per cent fat and 50 per cent lean; the fat beef animal 35 per cent and 50 per cent; the lean beef animal 25 per cent and 55 per cent. These compare with venison which has 2 per cent fat and 76 per cent lean and the warthog with 1·3 per cent fat and 82 per cent lean. 'The fat gains achieved by domestic animals,' says the Reading group, 'are the result of a combination of "over-feeding" high energy feeds, lack of exercise and genetic selection.'

Since 1955 animal fat consumption in the UK has increased by 10 per cent and meat and meat products provide just over a quarter of dietary fat intake now. The James Report wants us to reduce our fat intake by 10 per cent in the short term. Some of this can be achieved by eating less dairy produce, some by eating less meat fat, which in turn we can do either by eating less meat or by seeing that the meat we do eat is less fatty. The Reading group points out that not only do the younger generations dislike fat (unlike some of their ancestors) but that putting fat on an animal costs the farmer between five and seven times more than putting on lean meat, 'which points to a strong economic incentive for producers to reduce the levels of fat'. The Meat and Livestock Commission has a classification scheme for fat, with class 1 being leanest, class 5 fattest. Figures for 1976 showed that for class 1 beef carcasses the fat in excess of that consumed was 13·7 per cent of carcass weight; for class 3 (into which over 60 per cent of carcasses fall) it was 28·2 per cent; and for class 5 an enormous 46·1 per cent. Some of the fat which is trimmed from the carcasses ends up in manufactured meat products. Of the total fat supplied (excluding poultry) 50 per cent comes from the pig, 19 per cent from sheep and 31 per cent from cattle. Poultry is the least fatty farm animal we consume.

The production of excess fat involves both the incarceration of livestock to prevent exercise and large quantities of animal feed, often in the form of grain which would be better used if directly consumed by humans. The Reading group advocated a 24 per cent reduction in carcass meat consumption (most of which would come from those who already eat fatty meats) and a 43 per cent reduction of manufactured meat intake. The recommendations which we put forward later will not go down well with the food manufacturers or the intensive pigmen, but they will give a tremendous fillip to the extensive rearers of beef on the grass of our uplands. We shan't get the egret and peacock back onto the Sunday lunch table; but we can bring back something close to the lean wild bull.

More cereal; more fruit; more vegetables

It has taken the human race a long time to work out which foods contain what and how much we need of them to survive in a state of good health. Along with the guinea-pig, certain apes, a fruit-eating bat and the red-vented bulbul bird, man is one of the few species which has lost the ability to synthesize his own vitamin C, and without it he cannot survive. Man can live without animal products but not without a range of cereals, pulses and vegetables. (During the Depression in the USA, pellagra – dementia, dermatitis and diarrhoea – was widespread as a result of a diet of meat, maize and molasses.) The world derives about half of its supplies of protein by direct consumption of cereals, 20 per cent from pulses and 25 per cent from livestock products. Cereals and pulses furnish a good balance of proteins, and pulses are very useful as they are good nitrogen-fixers and thus fit very well into low-input rotations. The situation is roughly reversed in this country, with 62 per cent of dietary protein coming from animal sources (more from milk than meat) and the rest from plant sources. The James Report calls for a reduction in the consumption of livestock products and an increase in the consumption of cereals, vegetables and fruit. It is from these that we shall get the fibre, which in terms of grams consumed per person per day has fallen from around 27 in 1951 to 20 today. Obviously some foods are much richer in fibre than others. To provide 10 grams of fibre we need 23 grams of bran, 72 grams of rye crispbread, 105 grams of wholemeal flour, 108 grams of peanuts, 270 grams of carrots or 472 grams of strawberries. Brown bread, 196 grams of which provides 10 grams of fibre, compares favourably with white bread, of which we must consume 368 grams to get the same amount.

Consumption of both bread and potatoes has declined steadily since the last war. The Bird's Eye Survey of domestic consumption found that between 1962 and 1976 bread consumption fell 24 per cent. However it has been white bread that has been hit, and consumption of brown and wholemeal bread has steadily risen. During the same period potato consumption fell 34 per cent. The Reading group suggested that we would do well to return to a wider use of high-extraction flours of the types which were compulsorily used for all bread making between 1942 and 1953. To do so would increase the content of vitamin B, which is present in whole wheat, and retain high proportions of protein.

Clearly, if the public is encouraged to eat more vegetables and cereals, patterns of farm production will change. A fall in the consumption of dairy products and some meat products will lead to a reduction in the numbers of cows and pigs in particular. The reduction in the dairy herd will lead to land which presently produces cereals for feed being freed for other purposes (about 3·5 lbs of concentrate feed go into every gallon of milk produced). On the other hand if we are to use less fertilizer, then grazing of cattle may well have to be practised more extensively. It is this rearrangement of our use of land and energy that *Working the Land* describes.

3   *Animal Factory*

In the late seventies Pete King, the manager and producer of the reggae band Steel Pulse, boarded a plane to the United States. High up above the Atlantic he ordered chicken. Within five minutes of eating it he was violently ill. Nobody else ate chicken; nobody else was sick. It wasn't the first chicken to disagree with him and he decided to give up chicken. But abstinence just made the heart grow fonder. Out of curiosity he began to read about chickens and their production. Then he saw an advertisement placed by the famous author of *The Organic Poultryman*, Matthew Thomson. He was selling a Dorset breed which, if fed on whole grain, was alleged to lay heavily for eight or ten years (most battery chickens get the chop around their first birthday). 'So I bought a batch of twenty and stuck them at the bottom of my garden,' recalls King. 'I made some terrible mistakes at first, but I was smitten by then. Soon I had birds in the garage and before long they were right up against the bay windows.'

A couple of years ago King and his wife Debbie moved onto a ten-acre farm near Warwick, Nunhold Farm. A solid red brick barn houses hydroponic cabinets which grow the greenery for the birds, some incubators, a mechanical plucker and a workshop. Behind the barn are two fine old meadows, an orchard and a willow-fringed pond. Across the fields and around the pond stalk magnificent cockerels and hens. They are all Dorsets, some brown, some russet-black, others white. They are lusty self-confident birds straight out of the pages of Chaucer, their tail feathers held upright, breasts shining brilliantly, red combs as crisp and vivid as punk mohican haircuts, and thighs fluffed out like those of an Elizabethan courtier. There is no comparison between these birds – King is specialising in producing high quality table birds – and the 130,000 broilers kept in 'tight' houses just down the road.

We spent the day with King, observing his hens and learning

about their diet and the foibles of organic chicken rearing, and just before sunset we sat down to inspect an ex-cockerel in greater detail. To someone reared at the time when broiler chicken production was just taking off, this cockerel was a revelation. Certainly the leg meat was darker and tougher; it didn't simply collapse at the sight of stainless steel. But the real difference lay in the taste. King is a passionate lover of meat but he believes we should eat decent meat, meat which comes from animals which have been decently treated, fed on a wholesome diet and as far as possible kept away from the antibiotics and hormones which so many intensive rearers rely on. His table birds are reared on a diet of 'sunshine, water, grain, and greens'. The birds are provided with simple shelters and have access to meadows where they forage. He admits that his birds don't put on weight like broilers in intensive housing. And he makes no bones about the price of his birds. For a twenty-five-week-old bird he charges around 65 pence per pound. This compares with perhaps 35 pence per pound for the anaemic produce of the broiler house, where birds are killed between six and seven weeks old. King's birds may be more expensive but there is a demand which he cannot satisfy. When we dropped by Nunhold Farm in early July 1983 he'd just heard that Harrods could want 700 birds a week. Other enquiries were coming thick and fast, though King will probably supply the local market first.

Years in the cut-throat world of music have turned King into a real businessman. The scene at Nunhold may appeal to the romantic but the approach to rearing the birds is very scientific, so much so that the practices at Nunhold are now known as the 'King System'. The details need not concern us – either of the system of paddocks which adjoin the hen houses or the carefully controlled diet – but King is on the verge of supplying his system to other farmers. It is no coincidence that a couple of hundred miles south the Smith Brothers at Lower Bordean Farm in Hampshire, whom we shall meet shortly and whose free range egg farm is the biggest of its kind in Europe, are also establishing a system which they sell to other farmers. Both the Smith Brothers and King have the same problem: they can't produce enough of a good thing.

The animal population

Imagine a field with the following creatures in it: seven steers and heifers, one cow (past her prime and no longer any use to the dairy industry), 36 pigs, 36 sheep, 550 poultry and 15 rabbits. If you are an average meat-eating Briton with the average life expectancy, you will consume the contents of this field within your lifetime. In one way, however, we are giving a false picture. Most of these animals are not to be found in a field: modern farming has banished them and put them onto the factory production line. Our main concern in this chapter is with the pig and the hen, the two species which have suffered the greatest intensification, but it is worth giving a few figures to show the scale of meat eating in this country.

The animal population on farms and in factories is about 185 million, of which chickens account for 130 million. There are 58 million broiler birds in Britain and between 1977 and 1982 the average flock size increased from 23,039 to 27,375. Over half are in flocks of over 100,000 birds. The 1982 figure for laying hens was 45 million and nearly two-thirds of the laying flock are in units of greater than 20,000 birds. The battery system accounts for about 96 per cent of eggs laid; the deep litter system for 2 per cent and the free range system for 2 per cent. There is a lot of fuss at present about what a free range egg is, about which more shortly.

In 1982 there were over 8 million pigs in Britain, about three-quarters of a million of which were breeding sows. Approximately two-thirds of these sows are kept throughout their pregnancies in narrow confinement stalls – 'dry sow stalls'.

Attempts to raise sheep indoors under very intensive conditions have been disastrous and veal calves are the only other class of animal subject to severe restrictions under a crate system. The total number of cattle and calves in June 1982 was 13·3 million, but it is difficult to break this figure down because there is such a high degree of integration between the dairy industry and the beef herd, with about two thirds of the beef herd originating from the dairy industry. Systems of production range from the extensively grazed upland herds to intensively reared barley beef. Hormone implants are often used as growth-boosters with masculinizing and feminizing effects to beef up steers (castrated males), heifers and cast cows.

The total number of sheep and lambs in the UK was 33 million in 1982. Since 1980 the breeding flock has been increasing at the rate of about 3 per cent a year. This is not due to a sudden rush to the butchers' counters by consumers but follows the introduction of the EEC's sheepmeat regime. In order to encourage sheep production the Community fixes a guide price and makes deficiency payments to the farmer equal to the difference between the average market price and the guide price. There were periods during 1983 when farmers were receiving more in subsidies than they were getting from their receipts from the market.

Every minute of every working day 3,000 animals are slaughtered. Each year around a million lambs are estimated to die within a couple of days of birth of cold, starvation or exposure, and every year about 200,000 young calves, according to a Hoechst vaccination advertisement, die of diseases associated with stress.

Animal cruelty is an unsavoury subject and it is one which we aim to deal with quickly in order to concentrate on the alternative systems of animal husbandry. What we seek is an agriculture where the farm animal is decently treated, decently fed and killed as humanely as possible.

The vet's dilemma

Farm animals outnumber pets in Britain by ten to one, yet the amount of time spent by the veterinary profession on farm animals is just 27 per cent of the total. Vets, like doctors, sign an oath when they qualify, pledging that they shall do all within their powers to ensure that the welfare of their charges is paramount in their attentions. But what for the doctors is a Hypocratic oath has for the vets become a hypocritical oath, with the profession openly condoning practices of husbandry which at best are thoroughly uncaring and at worst downright cruel. Although there are many vets who are seriously worried about welfare on the farm, many condone the systems of intensification which cause such suffering.

We must be particularly concerned about the disease problems associated with intensive husbandry systems. A Reading vet, P.G.C. Dunn, outlined the problem in the *Veterinary Record* in 1980:

23

From a purely mathematical point of view the likelihood of
disease spread is increased [by intensification] and such
problems as atrophic rhinitis in pigs and calf pneumonia
serve to illustrate this. In order to overcome these problems
short term solutions such as antibiotic medication are
adopted. Too many intensively housed animals receive
antibiotics as a routine during their rearing period. This
simply perpetuates an unsound system and creates other
problems in terms of antibiotic drug resistance.

Dunn goes on to point out that the larger a dairy herd the
greater the risk of mastitis spreading; and the selection of high
yielding, fast milkers exacerbates the problem. (Since the war,
herd size has expanded rapidly. In 1982 the average herd
size was 55, and over two-thirds of the entire dairy herd runs in
units over 60 cows.) Dunn touches on the sensitive subject of
the vet's culpability:

Many have grown immune to the insidious development of
unsatisfactory husbandry conditions for our farm animals.
By tolerating such practices we support a system of animal
agriculture which is immoral. How many veterinarians feel
totally unconcerned at the sight of dry sows in confinement
stalls on a cold winter day? How many of us have a
completely clear conscience when we see four layers in a
battery cage?

One infamous illness which almost brought the poultry
industry to bankruptcy was Marek's disease. Having had
serious economic consequences during the 1930s the return to
small backyard flocks during the Second War led to the disease
causing little trouble. However in 1965 it once again hit the
broiler industry and flocks were destroyed on a massive scale
until a vaccine was developed in 1970. The seriousness of the
problem, according to P.M. Biggs, the Director of Houghton
Poultry Research Station, was due to the structure of the
industry and the concentration of poultry. To underline the
gravity of disease problems under intensive rearing conditions
J.D.H. Archibald, the managing director of the largest
breeding company in the country, wrote in *Poultry World* in
1978 that 'The rockiest road in the future is still likely to be
veterinary. The ceaseless fight to keep one jump ahead of the
next problem, on top of the present one and maintain sufficient

interest in the last one to prevent regression, is not going to change.'[1]

The view that intensification has gone too far is not confined to maverick vets. Here is Mr David Drummond, a MAFF chief veterinary officer, addressing a meeting of the Animal Diseases Research Association in 1980:

> The creation of large intensive livestock units in the UK has added to the industry's potential disease control difficulties and could make future slaughter and compensation policies prohibitively expensive. . . . We have some units of more than 10,000 pigs. In Europe, some producers have 50,000, while in the States some beef lots contain 250,000 cattle. Should foot-and-mouth disease strike such units, the effects could be quite catastrophic, resulting in the massive manufacture of concentrated virus with a fallout spread over vast areas.

Drummond concluded by telling his audience that money was no longer on tap for traditional eradication policies to deal with emerging diseases such as Aujeszky's disease of pigs.[2]

Of course, care of animals on the farm or in the factory is more the responsibility of the farmer than the vet. The vast majority of farmers in Britain do look after their stock as well as they are able; and many are appalled by intensive methods of husbandry. However, to reduce labour costs the number of animals per man has risen enormously. Colin Spedding, the highly respected Reading University Professor at the Centre for Agricultural Strategy, recently told a British Veterinary Association meeting that 'Livestock farming often appears to show little regard for individual animals.' He pointed out that, despite veterinary advances, mortality from birth to weaning in livestock is still very high at between 10 and 15 per cent (about ten times the comparable rates in Britain for the human population). The emphasis on keeping labour costs down has inevitably led to one man looking after more animals. Since the last war the number of ewes looked after by one man has risen from 200 to over 1,000, and one man can find himself looking after 60,000 battery hens.

Cages, stalls and pens

All but a small percentage of our eggs are produced by hens

confined in such small spaces that they spend their life unable to take two good steps forward or back. Egg and poultry meat production are no longer agricultural activities. A handful of agribusinesses hatch eggs and rear poults and only a tiny proportion of eggs and poultry meat is produced by independent farmers. It is an industry dominated by large companies. Superficially the business advantages of battery egg production seem obvious. Large numbers of birds can be kept in a small space (size is an important consideration when moderate agricultural land costs over £2000 an acre), lighting patterns can be controlled, eggs roll automatically into a trough and feed is delivered by mechanical hoppers.

The Egg Information Bureau publishes literature on the subject of egg production and their artist has managed the astonishing feat of getting hens to smile. Even Pete King's hens can't smile. And just down a couple of country lanes from King at the Royal Show the battery hens certainly didn't smile. The public were not allowed into the hen houses but a glass screen allowed them to peer in from one end. What is most noticeable on the approach to such houses is the foul smell; once inside it is the scraggy appearance of the birds, with breasts completely denuded of feathers and a stooped demeanour reflecting a life where wings have never been fully spread. The cages measure 16 by 18 inches and in most battery houses four birds per cage is the norm. The birds cannot do anything which they would normally do if allowed to behave naturally: they cannot perch, fly, spread their wings or dust themselves. Cannibalism is not uncommon. Though the environment of the battery house is supposedly controllable – with birds often getting eighteen-hour stretches of artificial daylight to induce heavier laying – heatwaves like that of 1983 can be too much for the houses' ventilation systems to handle. Temperatures can rise as high as 120 degrees when it is in the 90s outside. During our July travels we heard of one poultry farm in Wiltshire's Shute Forest where all 9,000 birds in a hen house suffocated to death during one scorching night. The hens took two days to bury. It is birds housed in such conditions that produce nineteen out of every twenty eggs. Despite the industrialization of egg production the industry is in deep crisis. In June *Farmers Weekly* commented: 'Over-production, falling consumption and increasing imports have already resulted in a prolonged period of depressed prices and this latest price cut of 3p a dozen on the larger egg sizes brings total returns to below the cost of feed alone for some producers.' The financial losses are expressed through the following equation, according to the NFU: when feed costs £155 a tonne, with consumption at 118 grams a day and egg yield at 276 eggs a bird a year, a dozen eggs will cost 29p to produce. And in early June that was exactly the price paid by many packing stations.

It is a matter for speculation whether the battery egg-producing hen leads a better life than the broiler bird reared for the table, though it is certainly longer. Michael Haines, Professor in the Department of Agricultural Economics at Aberystwyth, had this to say about the broiler business in his book *Farming Systems*: 'If maximum production is to be achieved, there is very little room in this system for error, and very little room either for sentiment, since more than in any other food production process which originated on the farm, poultry keeping has become a matter of economics rather than of husbandry.' Over half the country's 58 million broilers are in flocks of over 100,000 and the birds are reared under conditions of extreme crowding. The industry has expanded rapidly with rising demand and consumption per capita has risen from an average 5 lb a year in 1900 to 24 lb. At the beginning of the century it took forty weeks to rear a table bird; it now takes less than a couple of months. One can get two crops of a modern brand (and that is how the breeds are referred to now) between sowing spring barley and harvesting it. And what has been done for the chicken is being done for the turkey, the duck and the rabbit. (So far the goose has resisted attempts to intensify production.) Despite the recommendations of the Brambell Report that with indoor systems of turkey rearing birds up to 8 weeks should have at least 1·5 square feet of floor space each, from 8 to 12 weeks 2·5 square feet, and older than 12 weeks 4 square feet, these standards are persistently ignored. For example, according to the welfare group Compassion in World Farming, Britain's largest turkey producers, Bernard Matthews of Norwich, give the birds 1·25 square feet up to 8 weeks, 2·5 square feet from then to 16 weeks and a mere 3·5 square feet thereafter.

The pig, far more than the hen, is a creature which has a special place in man's affections. In his travels round England in the early nineteenth century William Cobbett observed the lot of the farmer and the farm worker. In *Rural Rides* he recalls a conversation with a turnip-hoer near Eastdean: 'In parting with him, I said, "You do get some bacon then?" "Oh, yes! Sir," said he, and with an emphasis and a swag of the head which seemed to say, "We must and will have that." I saw, and with great delight, a pig at almost every labourer's house.'

The pig had for centuries been important to the man on low wages. Traditionally the miners of Northumberland and Durham kept two pigs: one hanging from the larder ceiling, the other devouring the household scraps at the foot of the garden. Gerald Wibberley remembers the lot of many a small farmer in the years of the depression before the Second War: 'A family might have a pig to kill for themselves and perhaps a sheep and a few potatoes. They could buy nothing in and sacks had to do for raincoats.' Well, the days of the single pig eating the family garbage and later gracing the dinner table with bacon, sausage rolls, pig's trotters, hams and pork are now over, in this country at least. The pig, like the hen, has been subject to intensification. Eighty per cent of breeding pigs are in amalgamations (we can't call them herds) over 50 and half of all fattening pigs in this country are in amalgamations of over 1,000 animals. Of the three-quarters of a million breeding sows in Britain, two-thirds are kept throughout their pregnancies in narrow confinement stalls known as dry sow stalls. They lie on concrete floors and their rear ends stretch over a slatted floor which allows dung and urine to fall through. Lameness and spinal trouble are common. When the sow is due to farrow she takes about the only exercise she ever gets, apart from the walk into the abattoir: she is moved into a farrowing crate. A week after the litter is removed – at about three weeks – she is returned to the dry sow stall. When she comes on heat again she is served by a boar. Sows are often aroused by a drug called 'Boar-mate' and lined up in what the pigmen call 'rape-racks' to be served by the boar.

Traditionally piglets were weaned at eight weeks old and a sow would have two litters per year. But more pigs means more money. The suckling period has thus been reduced in intensive piggeries to three weeks. The piglets are transferred in many cases from the nipple into battery cages (tiered as with hens), from which they are later transferred to pens.

At the National Agricultural Centre's ideal pig unit sows

average five litters every two years. And of course the more piglets per litter the better. One of the more intriguing sights at the 1983 Royal Show was that of a gentlemen in a bowler hat painstakingly counting the number of nipples on a magnificent boar whose real talent hung very obviously elsewhere. What is required is a fourteen-titter if possible. Average number of pigs a litter is 9.

There are many different kinds of fattening pens. Some tolerable, others not. One has been developed in Ireland where pigs are kept in cages like chickens right up to their slaughter for bacon at 5 or 6 months. We shall return to the subject of pig rearing later in this chapter to show that free ranging makes economic sense but we can leave the topic for the moment with a few words from the Brambell Committee (1965): 'Pregnant sows should not be kept without daily exercise in quarters which do not permit them to turn round and, in any case, should not be tethered indoors.' Six years later the government translated this recommendation in its voluntary (i.e. ignorable) welfare codes: 'Where sows or gilts are housed individually they should be able to feed and lie down normally. . . . If tethers are used, they should not cause injury or distress.' New codes were published in 1983. The government at least recognised the serious welfare problems caused by intensive piggeries, even if it has failed to introduce statutory controls to alleviate the suffering.

The barbarism of the veal crate

'Volac have done an awful lot of good,' says ex-farmer Peter Roberts. 'They've taken the cruellest system and transformed it into one of the most ideal methods of intensive production.' Roberts says there are still shortcomings with the straw-yard system of rearing veal calves practiced by Volac, but such praise is quite something, coming as it does from the man who set up the welfare group, Compassion in World Farming. Volac is run by the vet Philip Paxman. The calves are reared in groups in straw yards rather than in the infamous crates which have for years deterred all but the most callous consumer from buying veal. Fortunately the use of crates for the rearing of veal is decreasing in this country. Under this system calves are confined in a cage in which they are unable to turn, often in darkness. 'White veal' comes from calves which have never been fed any roughage. In this country 20,000 calves a year are reared in 24 inch pens; rather fewer under loose-housed conditions. In the latter, calves are reared in groups of about twenty in pens which are relatively light and they are kept on straw rather than on slats. They can feed when they wish from milk machines and they can satisfy their desire for roughage by eating straw. Nevertheless, the Volac system is far from perfect. Calves are still kept subclinically anaemic (though not as pale as crated veal on the continent) and the process involves the traffic in very young calves (although many are reared by farmers under contract to Volac) and the use of 'replacement' milks delivered mechanically to animals weaned at a very early age. At the 1983 Royal Show one of Volac's specimens had to be replaced because it had ringworm, often a symptom of bad husbandry, and two of the calf units at the Royal were closed as salmonellosis had struck. Some of Volac's calves go for ritual slaughter (see below), the hind-quarters being returned to Volac for sale with conventionally slaughtered produce. Though 'welfare veal' is an advance on the crate system it still leaves much to be desired, and it is still mostly only available through butchers. Most restaurant veal remains continental and cruel.[3]

Travel and slaughter

When the time came for the coal miner to transfer the pig from the bottom of the garden to the larder the procedure was simple. The pig had a rope tied round its upper lip and was led into the garden. A neighbour would hold a bolt against the pig's forehead and a hefty blow with a mallet would send it into the pig's brain. The throat would be cut and the blood collected to make black pudding. The miner's wife scalded the skin and scraped away the coarse bristles. By the evening the pig would be hanging in the larder. Of course, death by this method could be either instant or long and agonized, according to the skill of the killer. Dreadful injuries could occur if the animal moved at the wrong moment and such methods were outlawed in the 1930s.

The slaughter of animals has changed much since then, and it is arguably even more cruel. Of the 1·4 million animals slaughtered every working day nearly all are bled to death by having their throats cut. First they have to be stunned, except where ritual slaughter is practiced. An article in *Farmers Weekly* in 1981 maintained that slaughter techniques used in British abattoirs are far from perfect: 'Recent tests have shown that many of the low-voltage electrical stunning systems used on pigs, sheep, and poultry are not as effective as they ought to be.' Some animals are conscious when their throats are cut.

The farmer who has spent his year tending his fat cattle or his sheep has no idea how the animals will fare when they go to the slaughterhouse. Particularly distasteful to most people is the ritual slaughter of meat for the Kosher (Jewish) and Hal Al (Muslim) market. With ritual slaughter the animal has its throat cut and is bled to death while fully conscious. Some of the meat which comes from animals which have been subjected to ritual slaughter finds its way back onto the gentile market. Religious slaughter also aggravates a prevalent abuse. Slaughter gangs are paid headage-rates and they brook no delays, among which may be counted the niceties of stunning. A gang seeing the Jewish method of ritual slaughter in operation may decide to ignore the legal requirement of stunning which applies to animals which are not bound for Jewish or Muslim consumption. After all, who is to know?

The transporting of animals, particularly when it takes them out of this country, is a cause for much concern. Mr A.G. Bains from the Marketing Department of the Meat and Livestock Commission told a Universities Federation Animal Welfare conference:

> During 1977 some 4·1 million cattle, 14·2 million pigs, and 11·4 million sheep were slaughtered. During the same year some 10·5 million store cattle [store stock are for fattening] sheep and pigs passed through livestock markets alone, and that takes no account of farm-to-farm transactions. A very high proportion of these animals will have moved by road. Some travel short distances while others travel the length and breadth of the country. For example, calves from Wales and the South West travel to East Anglia, the North of England and Scotland; fat pigs from Scotland to the North and Midlands; fat pigs from East Anglia to the South West; and fat sheep from Wales to the South West and the Midlands. . . . MLC estimates that some 10 per cent of all

finished lambs are damaged [the word is the meat trade's euphemism for 'injured' or 'hurt'] to a greater or lesser extent by bad handling, many sufficiently seriously to suffer a reduction in value. For pigs the incidence of damage is much higher, mainly from fighting, but this may not be so important economically except where stress impairs meat quality.

Most governments and agricultural ministers have been remarkably complacent about the export of live animals from this country. As long ago as the last Labour government John Silkin said he thought a ban would be a good idea. There has yet to be one and large numbers of farm animals continue to suffer in transit. According to the Farm Animal Welfare Coordinating Executive (FAWCE), 'virtually every unofficial, unheralded investigation reveals conditions of hardship, suffering and undue stress.'

The alternatives to factory production

There are few more astonishing sights in the country than the one that greets the traveller as he comes out from under a dense canopy of trees onto the hill north of Langrish in Hampshire. Beyond a field of winter wheat is a forty-acre field with ninety odd huts. From a distance it looks like an invasion of space invaders, each squat hut staring through its pair of windows at the passing travellers.

It is, in fact, the biggest free range egg farm in Europe. Lower Bordean Farm is run by two brothers, Michael and Andrew Smith, both of whom recently left careers in the army. And the farm is run with military efficiency. The Smiths are business men. They are in the free range business to make money, something which the big battery men are having a lot of trouble doing at the moment. 'When we started up the locals thought we were weirdos. They don't now, as they can see we are making money,' says Michael Smith. Not only are the Smiths making money, they employ five people on their forty acres, roughly the number one might expect to find working a fifteen-hundred-acre farm in the East Midlands cereal belt.

In 1978 the Smith family discussed the idea of getting hold of a farm. Michael had wanted to be a farmer when he left school but instead he joined the army. In 1978 he decided he'd leave the army within four years and set up in a soft fruit and vegetable business in Gloucestershire. But in 1980 six acres and the building at Lower Bordean came up for sale. The family bought it and put the six-acre field down to pick-your-own gooseberries, redcurrents, loganberries and blackcurrants. Michael Smith came home in 1981 and bought seventeen hens 'for self-sufficiency'. The hens produced more than the family could eat so they sold the surplus. Soon they were selling all the eggs: 'Everything must pay its way here.' So they bought another fifty hens, then another fifty. . . . By Christmas 1981 Michael Smith was running three hundred birds on his own. An adjacent twenty-seven-acre field came up for sale. This was bought, ploughed and sown with spring barley and a grass undercrop ready to take beef. Andrew Smith left the army in April 1982 and another ten acres came up so they bought that too. From then on it was expansion all the way. They bought some fifty-bird houses for £325 each and then designed their own ninety-birders. These are built for them by D. Mears of Northants for around £450 a piece. The manufacturer now builds them under licence to the Smiths and the Smiths sell them to other farmers. When Michael Smith took one of us round on a hot July morning in 1983 there were 6,500 birds in 85 houses. They were getting another thousand at the end of the month. Nearly all the hens are russet coloured Shaver 585s, a type of Rhode Island Red. The hens are bought in at point of lay (twenty weeks old) and kept for fourteen months. They are free to roam around the fields every day of the year (twenty-five Welsh Black sheep keep the turf down for them) and are locked up at dusk every day. It is difficult to imagine healthier looking hens. There have been no disease problems, the birds all have their full complement of feathers and they average a lay rate of about 75 per cent (i.e. 3 eggs every 4 days). The eggs are collected by hand and carted back to the farmstead on an Argocat, a low ground pressure vehicle.

In July the Smiths were producing 36,000 eggs a week, not nearly enough to satisfy demand. As well as local shops, Sainsburys and the Cooperative now sell Smith eggs. 'And if we can get hold of the land we'd like to have three-quarters of a million birds laying under our system in three years time.'

One of the major problems with the big battery units is the disposal of chicken manure. But not here at Lower Bordean.

'Our hens are putting down about sixty units of nitrogen (a unit equals one hundredth of a hundredweight) an acre each year,' says Michael Smith. 'We're thinking of running the hen business on a rotation. Say five years of hens, followed by two years of winter wheat or barley.' And the hen manure will be worth about £25 an acre for the corn crop if valued against bought in fertilizer.

The Smiths have a lot of small 'satellite' farms. The farms buy houses and equipment from the Smiths and then sell back their eggs. Clear-headed commercial men that they are, the Smiths have a legal contract which specifies to the satellite farmer exactly how he must look after his hens.

So what of the price of these eggs? When we visited the farm the retail price of pullet eggs was 55p per dozen; for size 5 it was 70p per dozen; for size 2, 90p per dozen; and for size 1, 95p per dozen. The same week the Eggs Authority listed retail prices in the South-East of England as 48p per dozen for size 5 and 72p per dozen for size 1. The Smiths' eggs thus cost about a third more than standard battery eggs.

The national individual average for egg consumption has been steadily declining. Between 1962 and 1976, according to (appropriately) Bird's Eye, egg consumption fell 13 per cent in this country. The 'Go Smash an Egg' campaign was launched by the Eggs Authority to attack the decline in consumption with, in the words of the Authority, 'a clear objective of making eggs more relevant to contemporary society'. Whether pictures of Billy Connolly and other celebrities attacking eggs have arrested the decline it is too early to say. In any case, shame on them for having allied themselves with this disgusting industry. Of rather more relevance to contemporary society is the price of the weekly shopping basket. The average Briton eats just over three eggs a week which means he spends (at July 1983 prices) 21p if they are battery eggs or 26p if they are the Smiths'. Five pence each week seems a small price to pay for supporting a humane system.

In September 1983 Michael Joplin, the Minister of Agriculture, found himself opening the Thames Valley Egg Packing Station at Lambourne Woods in Berkshire, and he had high praise for the egg industry: 'The egg industry has been remarkable for technical innovation and enormous increases in efficiency.' That depends on how one measures efficiency. In terms of productivity per man, yes, the egg industry is highly efficient. But we can look at it another way: isn't it better for five people to get useful and profitable employment from 6,500 hens, rather than just one person from 60,000? Free-ranging has implications well beyond animal welfare.[4]

Half of all the meat consumed in the world comes from the pig. Like the poultry industry, pig producers receive less state support than the rearers of ruminants. The excellent weekly paper *Farming News* highlighted the problem in July 1983. 'Costings of the 154 farms included in the Cambridge Pig Management Scheme show an average loss of £10.26 for every £100 of pig sales in the six months to March 31. When compared with those for the previous winter the costings show a 30 per cent rise in both feed and labour costs, the two largest inputs on a pig farm.' Losses varied between farms. The twenty most profitable farms made over £6 for every £100 worth of sales, the twenty least profitable losing £45. In an article immediately beneath the one carrying this grim report was the news that despite the depressed markets pig numbers continued to rise.

Pig finishing for pork and bacon is a perfect example of how precarious a farming system is when large quantities of feed have to be bought in, especially from abroad and with high import taxes. Between August 1982 and March 1983 the cost of feed wheat rose from £106 to £129 a tonne, barley from £100 to £118 and manioc from £150 to £165, while the cereal import levy on third country maize in February 1983 was £64 a tonne out of an ex-store price, tax paid, of £150 a tonne. Faced with such rising costs and with falling profit margins, the natural instinct of the farmer is to produce more rather than less, to get himself out of trouble. A July 1983 pig supplement in *Farmers' Weekly* had the following messages for the pigmen: maintain herd numbers, improve the conversion efficiency of feed to meat, keep the suckling period short. However, one page of the supplement was devoted to comparing free range to intensive piggeries. Taking these results together with those of Paul Carnell, in the study he produced in 1982 for Earth Resources Research Ltd, and those of Michael Boddington of Wye College, we find that outdoor pig production is a perfectly viable alternative to the intensive piggery, with all its problems of waste disposal, pollution and, often, cruel confinement.

Having compared outdoor and indoor herds in the 1960s Boddington was able to conclude that 'pigs kept outdoors are in no way less profitable than those kept intensively.' Whilst the indoor system was more productive and the numbers of litters and piglets reared per sow were lower outdoors, these 'inadequacies' were more than compensated for 'by the low costs incurred in terms of labour, sundry, housing, and other charges so that in the final analysis the surplus achieved, however measured, compares more than favourably with the performance of the indoor herd.' However, as Carnell notes, outdoor production has gradually lost favour with farmers and it seems that only one in twenty sows is kept outdoors today. Nevertheless he already perceives a revival of interest: 'Rapidly rising capital costs, augmented by high interest rates, together with changes in outdoor methods which appear capable of greatly improving performance, underlie this revival.'[5]

A study conducted by ADAS and the Meat and Livestock Commission (MLC) in 1979-80 showed stocking densities of 6·5 an acre, giving gross margins per sow of £150 a year and gross margins per hectare of £2400. (Professor John Nix's Farm Management Pocketbook gives a gross margin for a breeding sow in 1982 as £151.) A 1972 ADAS report considered that (to quote *Farmers Weekly*) 'a well run outdoor pig unit could make a major contribution to farm income in its own right and also benefit the farm rotation indirectly. But light free-draining land was a prerequisite to success.'

At a 1981 meeting of the Universities Federation for Animal Welfare at Wye College, Hedley Hawkins of Baxter Parker Ltd explained why his company specialised in outdoor pig rearing. It was formed in 1977 by Baxters the butchers and the Favor Parker feed firm, the object being to supply Baxters with pigs for their 400 shops and Parkers an outlet for feed. The company has 2,000 sows and fattens nearly 40,000 pigs a year. The company has four extensive and one intensive weaner production units (weaning can take from three to eight weeks; once weaned the pigs go through the finishing process where they are taken up to pork or bacon weights). When they are about 55 lb the weaners from both extensive and intensive production units are transferred to intensive straw rearing units.

Careful monitoring has enabled the company to compare the

efficiency of intensive and extensive breeding units. The capital costs of intensive units are much higher: £1300 per sow housed compared to £346 per sow for extensive units. And the running costs on a 350 sow unit in intensive conditions are approximately £6000 a year more than for outdoor pigs. Hawkins concluded that 'extensive breeding can be profitable, provided the soil type is right, the level of stockmanship is of high calibre, and careful performance records are kept so that management can identify problem areas and take action to correct them immediately.' Skill and fine husbandry are evidently the key to free ranging pigs successfully.

Action – when?

In 1981 the House of Commons Agriculture Committee submitted a lengthy report on 'Animal Welfare in Poultry, Pig and Veal Calf Production'. The Committee's report has been accepted by government 'in principle' but in practical terms it has been ignored. The sooner the Committee's recommendations are given statutory credence the better for huge numbers of poultry, pigs and calves. The main recommendations were these:

* That the rearing of veal calves in crates be banned. Meanwhile the catering trade should be convinced of the desirability of loose-housed veal and meat should be labelled so that the public knows what it's buying.
* That all veal calves be given solid feed after two weeks.
* That close confinement of pregnant sows be phased out.
* That battery cages for hens be banned after a warning period of five years.[6]

Another urgently needed reform concerns labelling. Food labelling is often deceptive and egg cartons provide an excellent example of how a cruel industry seeks to hoodwink members of the public into believing that they are consuming the produce of humane farming. 'Country Fresh Eggs Direct from the Farm' proclaims the 'Oasters' egg carton. Oasters is the trading name of Fridays Ltd, Chequer Tree Farm, Cranbrook, Kent. It is a battery farm, though one wouldn't suspect that from the picture on the label: a horse, smiling benignly like the Egg Information Bureau hens, pulls a cart of loose (not even baled) hay. It stands in the shadow of a thatched cottage and beneath its feet peck free range hens. To complete the rural idyll a happy farm girl chats to the man on the cart. Such labelling is both deceptive and dishonest, and it is imperative that the Trading Standards Offices enforce the legislation which is designed to prohibit such practices. Peter Roberts, who has in vain tried to get action from the Trading Standards people, is convinced that their reluctance to prosecute stems from their fear of taking on the Eggs Authority, MAFF and the NFU.

Alan Long, an honorary research advisor to the Vegetarian Society, is adamant that 'culpability for cruel systems of husbandry lies as much with the consumer as the producer.' The problem, of course, is that consumers often have no idea how the meat has been reared, and they will do so only when statutory obligations force the meat trade to label its products properly. There is a huge difference between a proper beef bull – an Angus, a Limousin, a shorthorn – reared on the hills from a suckler herd and a dairy bred cross, taken from the cow at birth and reared on concentrates indoors. There is a great difference between the calf reared in a loose-house system and fed roughage in natural daylight, and one kept for its brief life in solitary confinement and darkness. And though the egg of a battery hen is of a shape and colour which can't distinguish it from the produce of straw yard or free range hens, the method of production of the former is profoundly objectionable to most people. It is of great importance that the consumer has a choice, and ironically it is the recognition of how such choice might be exercised that has persuaded the heads of the meat departments in many big stores not to stock meat which is labelled as free-range or organically produced. One of our sources in the meat trade explained why: 'The butchers are scared because if they start labelling beef as "suckler-bred Angus" or "organically farmed beef" the housewife will ask "So what's wrong with the rest of the stuff?"' The consumer, if he or she considers intensive methods objectionable, should be able to sit down with a clear conscience when the top is sliced from the egg or the knife plunged into the roast pork.

A National Opinion Poll conducted just before the 1983 general election found that:

* 88 per cent of those questioned favoured the reform of factory farming.

* 90 per cent wanted laws to give factory farm animals freedom of movement to turn round, groom themselves and stretch their limbs. Sow stalls, tie stalls and veal crates would all have to go.
* 75 per cent wanted a ban on the live export of farm animals.
* 77 per cent wanted a ban on ritual slaughter.

If there is any one theme which runs throughout this book, and which runs through all the different aspects of farming from welfare to the curbing of surplus production and the over-use of oil-based fertilizers, it is that there are limits. Unless the farming industry recognises and defines these itself, the job will be done for it by a concerned public and Parliamentary legislation. It has to be recognised that if the price of increasing the productivity of a pig or a hen is inhumane incarceration then that price is unacceptable.

4 Muck and Straw: The Parable of Waste

The small Yorkshire town of Otley is solidly anchored beside the River Wharf, one eye squinting north to the high fells whence the waters come, the other glancing east to the rich arable plains through which the river flows to join the Humber. Where the Wharf begins there is nothing but heather and bilberry, the rain-sodden peat hags of the Pennines and the hardy black-faced sheep. The river gets its first glimmer of cereal crops as it rounds the bend at Otley. The Farnley Hall estate stretches from the bankside opposite Otley to the hills some five hundred feet above and to the north. It is a fine mixed farm.

Nicholas Horton-Fawkes spent twenty years working in the textile industry in Halifax before he decided to manage his estate full-time. Of his 3,000 acres he farms 1,200. The rest is tenanted to thirteen families, most of whom run small dairy businesses. Horton-Fawkes talks quietly and modestly about his farm. 'We're not doing anything special here,' he suggests.

His estate is far from easy to farm. The land is very variable and ranges from the sheltered fields in the valley bottom, hemmed in by hedges and woodlands, up to small meadows where the lines of the limestone walls are only broken by the occasional wind-swept ash tree. And the climate in this part of Yorkshire is as variable as the topography. Apart from the constraints of nature, circumstance has left him with two blocks: 600 acres by the river and around the magnificent Hall, and 600 acres on the high tops. The upland block is all down to grass. A herd of 130 brown and white Ayrshires – 'they're hardy and they suit low input farming systems,' says Horton-Fawkes – graze the uplands along with sheep. The lowland block is run as a mixed arable and sheep unit. In addition the farm fattens store cattle. Then there are 360 acres of mixed woodlands which employ one woodman and yield a clear profit of around £8000 a year. There's also a small fish farm making use of some of the four million gallons of water which pour out of Lindley Wood reservoir each day.

It was a cool blustery afternoon in early August when we left the Hall – well nourished on pigeon pie – and headed for the grazing meadows on the top. The Ayrshires were wending their way to the dairy and one of the seven workers was spreading muck on the grass. 'We're geared towards the maximum utilization of all our grass,' says Horton-Fawkes. 'Fertility is essential so we return all our animal and crop residues. Since we started our improvement programme we've doubled our stocking rates. It's the stock that's improving the land for us and each year we need less grazing land because of that.' In 1983 the farm took two cuts of silage off 350 acres. Some fields get a third cut and many of them provide grazing in the early spring and late autumn as well. 'We've spent a lot of time working on these upland grasslands,' says Horton-Fawkes. 'We've drained, we've reseeded, and we've experimented with different mixtures.' And it shows. A glance around the hillside at other fields some 750 feet above sea level reveals the familiar sight of rush-infested meadows, poor grass growth and low stocking densities. 'We have to be very commercial,' says Horton-Fawkes, 'otherwise we couldn't have a £250,000 turnover.'

If Horton-Fawkes owes his attitudes towards making a living from land to anybody, it is not to the high yield proponants of the fertilizer companies or ADAS, it is to Sir George Stapledon and Dr E.F. Schumacher, who argued that if man is to survive he must find ways of producing goods and services that are sustainable. The massively profligate use of oil-based fertilizers and the huge waste of such products as muck and straw are the antithesis of what Stapledon and Schumacher argued for. And Horton-Fawkes, who invited Schumacher up to Otley to give talks to local people, is putting into practice the business of sustainability. The high yields of his upland grasslands are not the result of huge doses of bag fertilizer. While many dairy farmers will put anywhere from 250 to 400 units of nitrogen down per acre, the most Horton-Fawkes uses each year is 120 on conserved grasslands (silage and hay) and 100 on the grazing fields. Furthermore he's not using straight nitrogen but nitrochalk and Chilean nitrate, two compounds which won't harm the biology of the soil.

There is, as many a Yorkshireman will tell you down the road in the industrial West Riding, brass in muck. But spreading it is just one aspect of sustaining the soil fertility at Farnley. On the lowland block an almost traditional rotation means that use of bought-in fertilizers is kept to a minimum, the soil is maintained in good fettle, and little food needs to be bought in to fatten the sheep or get the cows to produce decent milk yields.

The famous Norfolk Four Course arable rotation was devised in the eighteenth century and enabled land to be cropped continuously without reducing its fertility. In its classic form it consists of a first year of winter wheat, a year of turnips (which are fed to sheep) and a year of spring barley, undersown with clover which is grazed by sheep in the fourth year. The impoverishing effects of the two cereal crops are offset by the nitrogen-fixing properties of the clover and the manuring of the sheep. The Farnley rotation is not so rigid as the Norfolk Four Course but it's based on the same principle of enhancing soil fertility. 'Each autumn we look at the market,' says Horton-Fawkes, 'and decide what's best for the next year. We might have four years of grass, followed by a couple of years of winter wheat or winter barley, then a year of spring oats and a year of roots. But it varies.' The roots are particularly important in the rotation. They are geared to supplying feed for the sheep from the time when the grass dies back in autumn through till the early spring bite. Kale, rye, rape and soft turnips can all be seen on the land below the Hall. Not only is the rotation keeping the soil fertile, it enables the most effective use of the land. For example after a field of winter barley is combined in late July, a rape crop can be sown in August and fed to the sheep before the field is resown with spring corn.

Much that is happening on these slopes above Otley is relevant to how we shall farm for the next hundred years. There is no waste; none of the straw is burnt; all the muck is returned to the land. Chemicals, both in the form of fertilizers and pesticides, are used sparingly. Inputs of feed, for the sheep, the dairy herd and the store cattle, are all low, yet Horton-Fawkes's gross margins compare favourably with the high-input/high-output men. Apart from any considerations of the long-term health of the soil, it makes good economic sense to keep inputs down. Fertilizer prices will go through the ceiling soon; and as far as many livestock men are concerned, feed prices already have.

Sunshine versus oil

The Norfolk Four Course Rotation provided the farmer with something as near to a closed system as he could hope to have. The sun provided the energy to grow the corn, the roots and the clover. The sheep ate the roots and returned nitrogen and other elements to the soil and the clover took nitrogen from the atmosphere and converted it into a form available for plant consumption. The farmer sold his crops and the meat from sheep. It was never a way to get rich quick; but it was a way to survive the decades and the centuries. The system recognised its limits and worked with the principles of nature rather than against them.

At the beginning of the nineteenth century the Fens grew nothing but oats. However by the 1830s, after much draining work and the use of natural fertilizers, the fens were growing wheat as well as anywhere in the country. The natural advantages of the four course rotation could be enhanced by the use of fertilizers to supplement the good work of the sheep and the clover. Between 1852 and 1854 the firm of Messrs Gibbs sold over £5,000,000 worth of Peruvian guano (the dung of sea-fowl). This was good both for Messrs Gibbs and for the farmers whose arable yields shot up. But guano, like today's muck, was bulky and far from easy to spread on the fields. Soon after the first oil wells started delivering the black gold which paved the way for the motor age, the scientists found ways of turning it into fertilizer. By a relatively simple petro-chemical process oil and natural gas could be converted into small white granules of nitrogen fertilizer which could be conveniently packaged in hundredweight bags and spread on the fields at great speed.

Of course, the supplanting of animal manures by the 'artificial' fertilizer has taken many years, but it has revolutionised farming. The old rotations could be abandoned, soil fertility could be maintained by bag fertilizers rather than by stock and nitrogen-fixing plants, and the farmer no longer needed to 'waste' land under fodder crops. Man's ingenuity, it seemed in the golden years of the fifties and sixties, had provided us with the perfect means of getting high yields in perpetuity. Some of the other changes which went with the switch from the 'manure and sunshine' diet to the petrochemical diet were worrying. Disease problems, formerly countered by rotating crops, increased dramatically, so the chemical companies had to develop herbicides, fungicides, nematocides and pesticides (which kill, respectively, weeds, fungi, nematode worms and other animal pests). But, everything considered, we had done pretty well. Yields increased dramatically and they continue to increase. The farmers prospered and the consumers were never faced with any shortages.

But with the petrochemical revolution came great changes in the structure of the industry. In the areas where arable crops grow best – in the great belt which runs up the east coast from London to the Firth of Forth – farmers could forsake stock and concentrate on what their land seemed to be best at: not growing fodder crops for sheep on a rotational basis but producing continuous cash crops like barley and wheat. Livestock rearing became concentrated more and more in the west and on the hills. Today, for every 100 acres in Cambridgeshire and Bedfordshire there are 63 acres of cereals, 10 acres of grass and 12 acres of oil-seed rape and vegetables. For every 100 acres of Somerset and Devon there are just 14 acres of cereals, 73 acres of grassland and less than an acre of rape and vegetables. Acre for acre there are 16 times more dairy cows in the two western counties, 4 times more beef cattle and 10 times more sheep.

The Norfolk rotation was sustained through recycling. Nothing was wasted. Sugar beet tops and other crop residues were spread on the land; every ounce of arable muck ended up in the soil. The straw from the wheat, barley, rye and oats was either eaten by stock or used as bedding. Either way it was returned to the land and had a valuable effect on soil structure. Such careful recycling mimicked, as well as the farmer was able, the recycling of energy and elements found in natural systems. The switch to using petrochemicals from our fossil fuels has broken the pattern. As one American ecologist said recently, we no longer eat potatoes made from the sun, we eat potatoes made from oil.

But not for ever. According to the government's latest figures North Sea oil and gas reserves will start to decline in the 1990s.

We shall not suddenly run out of fertilizers, but nitrogen will gradually get more and more expensive. And while the price of nitrogen shoots up so will that of phosphate. The world's phosphate supplies are found in large quantities in just a small number of places, often in politically unstable countries. The war that has been raging for nearly a decade in the Western Sahara between the indigenous desert people and the invading Moroccans has much to do with the west's dependence on the country's phosphate reserves. Should pro-west Morocco fail to win the war, there is no guarantee that the Sahrawis will sell us the fertilizer. And unfortunately the world's sea birds are unable to produce guano at anything like the rate to satisfy our present demand for phosphate.

However, there is no need for despair. Oil may be running short and phosphate supplies are uncertain, but the sun remains as faithful as ever. With the help of our farmstock and the judicious rather than reckless use of 'artificial' fertilizers, our farmers will be able to produce as much food as we need for the next centuries. Furthermore, there is no question of turning back the clocks. Horton-Fawkes and other farmers whom we look at in more detail in the next chapter are producing decent yields using the sun and their stock.

Muck: the waste

Britain's farm animals produce huge quantities of manure, only about a third of which is used. The rest is dumped, wasting valuable nutrients and often causing severe water pollution. It has been calculated that around 190 million tonnes of manure are produced every year. According to Dr R.D. Hodges of Wye College, this amount of manure would supply approximately 1,280,000 tonnes of nitrogen (N), 312,000 tonnes of phosphorus (P) and 859,000 tonnes of potassium (K). There are more than 7 tonnes of manure available for every acre of cropland and Hodges suggests that if calculated on the basis of a nutrient content similar to that of farmyard manure, which would be a low estimate, the nutrients available from the 7 tonnes would be 42 kg nitrogen, 22 kg phosphorus and 49 kg potassium. (A two-ton-per-acre crop of wheat removes from the soil: 41 kg N, 4 kg P and 41 kg K.)

Manure comes in two different forms. There is farmyard

45

manure (FYM), which is a mix of dung, urine and straw bedding. FYM varies according to the richness of the animal's diet, the amount of bedding used and the way in which it is stored before spreading. FYM is the old-fashioned stuff. With the introduction of more intensive systems, the trend away from straw bedding and the need for cheap ways of dealing with large amounts of excreta, liquid manure and slurry (excreta, urine and water) have become the main currency. It is said that the amount of slurry produced each year in Britain would cover all six lanes of the M1 between London and Leeds to a depth of forty-two feet. It is this liquid product that is causing the greatest problems for farmers. In areas like Humberside, where there are massive intensive piggeries and not enough land to dispose of the wastes, the nuisance to local people has become very severe. In 1979 the Royal Commission on Environmental Pollution issued its seventh report. The Commissioners looked at the pig problem on Humberside and didn't like what they smelt: 'We are talking here of smells that are far removed from the "good country smell" of farmyard manure. The smell of pig slurry is highly offensive and penetrating.'[1]

The disposal of liquid slurry poses many more problems than that of FYM. If spread in wet weather most of it is washed away, resulting in polluted streams and rivers and run-off into drinking water supplies (fears about nitrate-related cancers are discussed in Chapter 5). And if applied to the land in dry weather the slurry can run straight through the cracks in the soil, again ending up in the water supplies.[2]

In 1983 a new agricultural society was established. It is known as RURAL – an acronym for the Society for the Responsible Use of Resources in Agriculture and on the Land – and it has set itself the task of finding better ways of reducing waste, encouraging rural employment, reducing our dependence on inputs such as fossil fuels and encouraging farmers to be more ecologically minded. The Council of RURAL reads like a Who's Who of rural politics. Its chairman is John Quicke of the Country Landowners' Association, its honorary treasurer is Prof Frank Raymond, former MAFF chief scientist, and the director is Dr Mike Wilkinson, *Farmers Weekly* grasslands expert. On the Council are Jack Boddy, farm workers' leader, Lord Middleton, president of the CLA, Eric Carter, director of the Farming and Wildlife Advisory Group,

Sir Ralph Verney, former chairman of the Nature Conservancy Council and David Stickland, the managing director of Organic Farmers and Growers Ltd. The NFU took a rather snooty attitude to the group when it set up, despite its eminent backing, but the seriousness with which RURAL views the agricultural situation today was very evident at its first meeting. Muck, not surprisingly, was high up on the agenda. Among those who talked about it were Dr B.F. Pain of the National Institute of Dairying, V.C. Nielson from ADAS's farm waste unit at Reading and C.A. Edwards of Rothamsted Experimental Station. The story they had to tell was one of profligacy and they put some figures to the problem.

Each year cattle in this country produce 4·31 million tonnes of dry matter excreta, pigs produce 0·73 million tonnes and poultry 1·12 million tonnes. Cattle manures can generally be spread on land – even if wastefully – but the handling problems posed by poultry and pig excreta are enormous.

At the RURAL meeting the scientists gave estimates for the percentage of land under various crops which received organic fertilizers: spring cereals 19 per cent; winter cereals 13 per cent; potatoes 42 per cent; sugar beet 29 per cent; other arable land 21 per cent; temporary grass 46 per cent; permanent grass 35 per cent.

Overall, this means under a third of our crops and grass receives any manure or slurry.[3]

RURAL is the brain child of Neil Wates, a former builder who now runs Bore Place, a dairy farm set amid the woody valleys of the Kent Weald. The slurry from the 300 dairy cows is fed through a bio-gas digester. Once the methane has been taken off, the digested slurry is stored in a big lagoon. Farm manager Stewart Crocker is appalled by how many farmers waste their slurry. 'Only a third is used on our farms,' he says. 'And of that most is spread unevenly.' Crocker estimates that the use of the Bore Place slurry saves the farm about £7000 a year, money which would otherwise have been spent on nitrogen. The digested slurry has the added advantage of having an extremely low pathogen content. The period of rejection by cows of grass treated with raw slurry is about a month; with the digested slurry it is only a few days.

Crocker recently went on a tour of China and the United States to study waste use. The Chinese, it seems, use every ounce of muck – both human and animal – in retaining the fertility of their soil.

Straw: burning issues

The visible signs of muck waste are not obvious. Green algal slime covering ponds and rivers and the odd seeping lagoon are all the public is likely to see. The occasional whiff alerts us to the intensive piggery and poultry farm, but it doesn't necessarily mean the manure is wasted. However, it's a very different matter with straw. Each year about 6 million tonnes of the stuff go up in smoke, and as *Farmers Weekly* put it in an autumn editorial, 'In 1983, cereal farmers have screwed it up.' The public had had enough, and so had the fire brigades. On one weekend the Essex fire brigade was called out over a hundred times to deal with fires out of control. The National Farmers' Union had tightened up its Burning Code but to little avail. The Fleet Street editorial writers all became experts on the problems of straw burning and the papers listed a grim catalogue of burnt hedges and woodlands, motorway accidents caused by smoke and polluted air. So strident were the calls for a ban that if one hasn't already been imposed by Parliament by the time this book comes out it soon will be.

Oliver Walston is a big farmer in Cambridgeshire. His regular columns in *Farmers Weekly* generally give the big arable farmer's point of view. But on the straw issue he sided with the public. 'It's time to put away the matches,' he wrote. 'It's time to stop burning straw. We have been lucky it has lasted as long as it has, but today straw-burning must join the long list of antiquated habits which litter British agriculture.' Walston has stopped burning on his farm, and it will cost him more to chop the straw and incorporate it into the soil, but he points out that the French and Germans hardly burn any straw and that in any case farmers should complain no more about a ban than industrialists who are forced to spend money to clean up their pollution.

While arable farmers up the east of the country were setting fire to their straw, livestock farmers in the west were travelling long distances to get winter supplies. Auctioneers Russell, Baldwin and Bright reported the 1983 market for straw as excellent. 'We have experienced the most exciting straw trade for many years,' their chairman told one farming paper. 'Demand has been exceptionally high from most parts of Wales as well as Herefordshire, Worcestershire and Shropshire.' So while over 6 million tonnes of the estimated 13 million tonnes goes up in smoke, farmers in the west are paying good prices for it. Again, the waste is a reflection of the rift between arable and stock.

Straw also has other uses. It can be burnt in straw burning boilers, and according to RURAL the straw which is now burnt could theoretically supply the total requirements of UK agriculture for crop drying, heating and lighting. Over 40 per cent of fuel directly used in agriculture goes on heating greenhouses, and straw would be ideal for that job, especially as much of the surplus is produced in the areas where most glass houses are found.

There is no doubt that a ban will cost the arable farmer money (it won't cost the mixed farmer any as he uses his straw) but there is also no doubt that the soil benefits from incorporation by a build-up in humus. Although few farmers practise incorporation in this country, 5 of the 8 million tonnes of surplus straw in France is treated in that way.

The wastage of muck and straw requires not a high-tech solution but common sense. We must get back to a more balanced system of farming, and in the chapters that follow we show some ways in which that can be done. Farmers can produce good yields with organic manures, careful rotations and the use of nitrogen-fixing plants like clover and lucerne. There is nothing old fashioned about this. Rather, the opposite is true. If nitrogen fertilizers ran out tomorrow what would happen to the corn men in Cambridgeshire and Bedford? Could they survive? One thing is sure: Horton-Fawkes wouldn't have to stop farming, nor would he stop making money. His sheep, his cows and his fatstock would make sure of that.

5   Coming off the Chemical Treadmill

'I come from the generation brought up on fertilizers,' says Richard Fry candidly. 'And when I became manager and Mr Wookey told me that we weren't going to use fertilizers or sprays I was quite frightened. And I was sceptical at first.' That was eight years ago.

Barry Wookey farms 1,700 acres of rolling downland around the Wiltshire village of Rushall. In 1970 he began weaning his fields off chemicals. 'We're trying to farm again,' he says. 'The present system is very wrong and even the whizz-kid farmers are getting worried about the chemical treadmill.'

'This is a modern, commercial farm,' says Fry as we pull onto the hill from whose crest we can see fifteen churches and the white horse of Pewsey Vale. 'Organic people are often seen as eccentrics. You know: a few cows, a few goats, a few hippies. Well I reject that!' Fry is a big, powerful looking man in his mid-thirties. He talks in a quiet, rolling Wiltshire accent, but his passion for the way he and his boss farm is very evident. As we wait for two fifteen-foot New Holland combines to rumble up the hill towards the winter wheat which is about to be harvested, Fry talks of the skill required to farm without chemicals. 'Taking a field off sprays and fertilizers is like taking a human being off drugs. It's as though the ground keeps saying "Where's the bag of nitrogen?" We've found that the longer our fields have been in organic rotation the better the crops.'

But how about diseases? Fry grins. 'This year one of the neighbours had every disease imaginable on one of his wheat fields. He'd got septoria, eyespot and all sorts, so he called in an expert to see what could be done. They had a look at his fields and then they had a look at my Maris Wigeon over the fence. They didn't find a thing in my field. And he was the one who was spraying!'

'We can keep our fields clean of weeds and disease-free by good husbandry,' explains Barry Wookey in the village pub.

'We should tolerate a certain amount of weeds. We have few problems. Sprays should be used like you use the fire brigade. You don't call the fire brigade to put out the sitting-room fire every night, do you?' Wookey maintains that if one grows decent crops organically their natural health will overcome disease problems. And indeed a trip round the farm confirms his view. Wheat, barley, oats – all are yielding well in clean fields. Wookey averages 2 tonnes an acre of hard wheat, which he mills himself. 'We're doing as well financially as the average chemical farmer. Not as good as the best; but the best will come down soon. In 1990 we shall still be getting our two tonnes an acre with low inputs and we shall be laughing.'

Wookey is scathing about the lack of research on low-input farming: 'We spend millions of pounds every year on research into chemicals and not a penny on sustainable systems.' The low-input farmers of the next century will not have ADAS or the Agricultural Research Council to thank for the know-how they will undoubtedly need. It will be the trials, errors and tribulations of farmers like Wookey that will establish the best practices.

While the Rushall wheat was coming off the downs and heading for the corn dryer and the mill, David Stickland was wheeling and dealing in a small office beside the station in Needham Market. He's the managing director of Organic Farmers and Growers (OFG), a cooperative which provides the sort of help that low-input men need but can't get from ADAS or firms like ICI. OFG buys produce from about seventy farmers, and markets and sells it. 'We handle anything,' says Stickland, whose farming experience has taken him as far away as New Zealand and Canada. 'Yesterday it was cattle and blackcurrants and I imported some worm casts from the Philippines. This morning I was selling pyrethrum. . . .'

The organic movement has often been accused of being both dogmatic and self-righteous, and the zealous and confrontatory propagandising by some elements within it has done the movement more harm than good. Stickland's cooperative is providing the sort of bridge required between the purists and those who know that they will have to forsake the chemical treadmill one day. Organic Farmers and Growers has two separate standards. The first is known as OFG 1, and food which falls into this category is 'organic' in the true sense of the word. No herbicides, insecticides, pesticides or other agrochemicals can be used. Crops can only be fertilized by manures, seaweed products, rock minerals (phosphates, potash and so on), and animal products such as dried blood and bonemeal. The only insecticides used for OFG 1 produce are the benign ones like pyrethrum, derris, nicotine and rotenone. Weeds and diseases are controlled by rotating crops, mechanical hoeing and, where possible, by biological control (by predatory insects like ladybirds on aphids, for example). Farmers are encouraged to include legumes in the rotation to provide nitrogen, and to use deep rooting crops which will bring trace elements up from the subsoil. When they can find time they are encouraged to grow a crop like mustard which can be ploughed in as a green manure. It almost goes without saying that the farmer will be a mixed farmer.

'One of the big problems for the low-input farmer today,' says Stickland, 'is that his fixed costs are so high.' (A farmer's fixed costs include his wage bill, machinery and its depreciation, and rent.) 'Even if he never gets out of bed he's still going to have to pay at least £100 an acre in fixed costs. And with wheat at around £120 a tonne he must get a tonne an acre just to pay off these costs.' Then the farmer must pay off the variable costs – of seed, fertilizer, sprays and feed. It was with this awareness of high fixed costs that Organic Farmers and Growers decided to devise a second grade. It is the informed pragmatist's best bet at the moment, and it is known as BFG 2. Its basis is biological farming methods topped up by the use of carefully chosen agrochemicals to help increase yields. BFG 2 farmers – Horton-Fawkes is one – can use, in addition to organic manures, nitro-chalk and Chilean nitrates of soda and of potash. For phosphate sources the farmer must use basic slag (a by-product of the steel industry), rock phosphate and single superphosphate. The use of limestone, chalk, and seaweeds is also allowed. Weed control can be done using non-residual herbicides like MCPA and MCPB. Similar insecticides to those used by OFG 1 farmers may be used. Livestock may not be treated with growth-promoting hormones, and antibiotics may only be used to combat disease in individual animals rather than as a blanket precaution against disease. They should be fed on forage crops grown to one of the two standards.

'Every farmer in the country should have one field down for

BFG 2 food production,' says Stickland. 'So when the day comes when they can't afford – for either economic or biological reasons – to carry on using artificial fertilizers and sprays, they will have acquired the skill to produce good yields without them.'

More and more farmers are coming off the chemical treadmill. Many who are not, wish that they could. 'The chemical manufacturers have really got us trapped,' said one of our farmers whose high yielding dairy herd grazed pastures which received over 300 units of nitrogen an acre. 'I'm on the treadmill at the moment. My overheads are enormous. I just can't afford to let my yields drop.' The chemical companies will do their best to make sure farmers stay on the treadmill.

There is an adage that this year's spray contains next year's disease. The chemical route, apart from being profligate in its use of non-renewable resources, 'tempts the worst in nature'. The disease will always be a step ahead, always evolving to outwit the latest chemical. In the long run it is better to control pests and diseases by the stealthy intelligence of good husbandry.

Fertilizers: money down the drain?

The two biggest inputs on British farms today are feed stuffs and fertilizers. MAFF's 1982 forecast for expenditure on fertilizers and lime was £808 million. To put this figure into context we can compare it with other expenses. Forecasts for expenditure on livestock was £175 million and for labour £1697. This means that fertilizers cost around half of the labour bill.

During the fifties and sixties fertilizers were very cheap. Only the most strong minded farmer was likely to resist using them generously on his fields. The oil crisis in the early seventies changed both the price of fertilizers and attitudes to how we use fossil fuels.

Professor Nix of Wye College provides estimates of how much a chemical farmer is likely to spend on fertilizers for various crops. For winter wheat yielding 5·75 tonnes per hectare he estimates that for each hectare the farmer will pay £42 for seed, £70 for fertilizers and £70 for sprays. For maincrop potatoes the farmer will spend in the region of £195 and for oil seed rape about £125 per hectare on fertilizers.

Despite the high prices which farmers must pay for their fertilizers, the manufacturers claim that they are in financial trouble at present. They will point out that although prices of fertilizer rose by 91·5 per cent between 1975 and 1981, this was low compared to other increases which affect the farmer. (For example, during the same period heating fuels rose by 234 per cent, tractors by 141 per cent and veterinary services by 119 per cent.) And now, they complain, prices are almost static. This, however, is not going to last.

Since the last war fertilizer use has rocketed and since 1950 it has increased at least eight-fold. In 1974/5 nitrogen fertilizer consumption was 979,000 tonnes. Six years later it was 1,335,000 tonnes.[1]

It has been the application of large quantities of fertilizer that has done most to raise yields on the farm. Thirty years ago 3·7 tonnes per hectare of winter wheat was considered a good yield. The average yield now is over 6·2 tonnes per hectare and new strains of wheat are selected for their ability to respond well to heavy doses of fertilizer. The record for winter wheat now stands at over 15 tonnes a hectare. The crop was given an astonishing 185 units an acre of potash, 125 of phosphate, 50 of magnesium and 260 of nitrogen. It was a futile experiment. Research scientists with foresight would be better employed investigating how little fertilizer they can get away with without significantly reducing yields rather than carrying out high-input/high-output experiments. Certainly, this sort of high-yield research does the farmer of the future no service.

The sheer magnitude of farmers' petrochemical dependence becomes apparent when one looks at the energy budget for agriculture. The Economist Intelligence Unit carried out a study for the European Commission on the amount of energy used by farms in the Community. A third was used directly on the farm, of which three quarters was in the form of petroleum products and the rest gas, coal or electricity. The other two thirds of the energy budget went on indirect consumption. Of this, 44 per cent went on fertilizer, 31 per cent on feedstuffs and 14 per cent on machinery. Fertilizer thus creates the greatest demand on support energy for farming.

Approximately 4 per cent of Britain's total fuel consumption goes on the farm. In addition to the 4 per cent used on the farm, processing, packaging and distribution of food takes up another

12 per cent of Britain's energy. Our high level of dependence on finite fuel resources is the cause of much concern among agriculturalists. The European Commission normally formulates its agricultural policies with a marvellous disregard to anything beyond the next financial year, but in its 1982 annual report it showed signs of unease at our farms' energy consumption, even posing the question, 'Would it be a solution to import larger quantities of certain foods from countries which produce them by extensive means, that is, with a low level of energy input?' Were it not for the tariffs and import levies we would undoubtedly be buying beef from the United States and Argentina where farmers practise low-input systems. The Commission Report almost says as much, though it suggests that to begin trading in such a way would create more problems that it would solve. It does however advocate the replacement of chemical fertilizers by biological ones.

One of the biggest problems with the application of chemical fertilizers is wastage through run-off. The Grasslands Research Institute carried out experiments which revealed that almost 80 per cent of the nitrogen applied to intensively grazed pastures is wasted. The research team found that from a perennial ryegrass sward receiving 420 kilograms of nitrogen per hectare only 7 per cent was recovered in animal products. (When *Farming News* reported this research it carried an article on the opposite page which began 'Producers with 18-month beef systems could expect an economic growth response from fertilizer rates as high as 400 kg of nitrogen a hectare – three times the average.' Is there any wonder farmers get confused?).

Of every pound's worth of fertilizer the farmer buys he can expect the rain to wash away a good fifty pence worth. Very occasionally nitrogen recovery may be as high as 70 per cent but this still means 30 pence is going down the drains. But it's not just the farmer who should be worrying. It's all of us. The build up of nitrates in ground water supplies is frightening both water authorities and the medical profession. According to many medical experts, over-use of nitrates in modern farming is causing stomach cancer in humans. One of the unfortunate features of the nitrate problem is the lag-time between the application of the fertilizers and their eventual arrival at the ground waters. It has been shown that nitrates move through the soil at the rate of about one metre a year so water authorities drawing water to the surface from wells twenty metres deep are finding nitrate levels which reflect fertilizer use twenty years ago. In some parts of Britain – notably East Anglia – levels of nitrate in the water already regularly exceed 50 parts per million and occasionally 100, the World Health Organisation's maximum permissable level for drinking water. However, as the use of fertilizers has greatly increased over the past two decades we can expect rising nitrate counts in our drinking water which will reflect this. Although medical evidence tying nitrates to cancers is not conclusive the authorities are determined that we should not be subjected to greater levels of nitrate-laced water than we are at present.[2]

The way in which we farm must ensure that nitrates are not leached out in such great quantities. This means much greater care must be taken with bag nitrogen. Farmers should try and shift away from the fast-release fertilizers like, for example, ICI's Nitram to ones which release their contents to the soil over longer periods and which are more likely to be taken up by the crop rather than by passing rainwater. Organically based fertilizers like those sold by Palmers of Peterborough are evidently preferable to the standard NPK fertilizers, both from the point of view of the crops and the ground water.[3]

The nitrate problem is going to get worse before it gets better. Everybody agrees about that. Greater care with the use of bagged fertilizer, lower application rates, the use of organically based fertilizers, and preferably organic manures, shallower ploughing and fewer spring crops will all help. In the meantime the water authorities will do what they can. Ultimately, however, it will be the balanced farm that will solve the nitrate problem.

The pest war

DDT is an organochlorine insecticide. It is even more persistant than fertilizer representatives and it stays around in the environment for enormous periods of time. It was fears about DDT that sparked off the environmental movement of the 1960s. Not only can the various -cides we use (pesticides, fungicides, herbicides, nematocides) upset the ecological balance of the country, they cost the farmer large sums of money, they are extravagant in their requirements of energy, they often cause the farmer more problems than they solve and they can be dangerous to those who apply them. Above all, pesticides exemplify how the manufacturers will do everything they can to make sure that farmers continue to buy and use their products.

Control over the use and distribution of pesticides is very lax in this country. The decline of the peregrine falcon and other birds in the 1960s as a result of DDT working its way along the food chain – from a dressing on corn to insects, to rodents and finally to the predators which suffered sterility and other problems – led to the setting up of the Pesticides Safety Precaution Scheme. The Scheme is a voluntary arrangement through which companies that are members of the BAA (British Agrochemicals Association) and the British Pest Control Association notify all their new products to MAFF's Advisory Committee on Pesticides. The Committee pronounces its opinion on the product and if all goes well it recommends on which crops it should be used and in what quantities. The Scheme relies on farmers using the products as directed and it can do nothing about the black market trade in non-approved chemicals.

In 1969 the Committee recommended to the government that the use of persistant organochlorines – DDT, aldrin, dieldrin and endrin – 'should cease as soon as practicable'. The government agreed. Yet a MAFF survey found that between 1975 and 1979 the amount of DDT used was actually 5 per cent higher than during the period 1971-4. The Royal Commission on Environmental Pollution confirmed that farmers were using greater quantities of dangerous pesticides rather than less, and in 1978 Joyce Tait, a researcher at the Open University, carried out a survey among 84 Lincolnshire farmers who grew cabbages, sprouts, cauliflowers and broccoli, and every one admitted using DDT.

The amount of -cides used in Britain continues to increase. It is thought that by the mid-seventies 99 per cent of soft fruit, 99·5 per cent of cereals and 98 per cent of potatoes, sugar beet and field beans were receiving pesticide treatment. Very few of the pesticides used are selective. In other words they kill many more than the target species, and in many cases they kill species that are beneficial to the crop. The lack of information in the early days of pesticides led to farmers adopting a very cavalier attitude to what were very dangerous substances if misused.[4]

The rumpus over 2, 4, 5-T has been a typically difficult case. This is a herbicide which contains small traces of the highly toxic dioxin, a substance known to be carcinogenic and to cause birth defects. (Vietnam provided the perfect laboratory as dioxin impurities were present in Agent Orange, the defoliant dumped in huge quantities over the forests. Both local Vietnamese and American troops have suffered high rate of cancer as a result.) The farmworkers' union has for years campaigned for a ban on 2, 4, 5-T and it is already banned by many local authorities.

It is no longer just the environmentalists, the doctors and the trade unions who are worrying about the high levels of pesticide use. The Royal Commission on Environmental Pollution, a body considered so prestigious that even the British Agrochemicals Association reacted to its findings with uncharacteristic restraint, said the following:

> Pesticides are by design biologically active and hence hazardous chemicals; however stringent the tests applied to them, there is the possibility of unforeseen and unforeseeable effects. They should be used with care, in the minimum quantities needed for effective pest control, and increasing usage should be questioned.

The wise use of chemicals, said the Commission, could not be ensured by the restraining effect of cost.

The Commission pointed to the alarming rates at which pest species developed resistance to the chemical armoury.[5] In 1954 there were just 25 species resistent to pesticides. In July 1980 the Food and Agriculture Organization (FAO) calculated that there were 432 resistant species. This is now the most serious problem in the pest war, according to George Cooke, former chief research scientist at the Agricultural Research Council. He has suggested that the amount of pesticides used by farmers in this country could be reduced a thousand-fold and still be more effective. As the pest outwits the chemical the farmer who stays on the spraying treadmill tends to spend more and more in the war against it. Professor Nix's figures for crop costs show just how expensive the pest war has become. The figures here show the amount a farmer will pay on pesticides as a percentage of his gross margin (i.e. the price he gets for the crop less the cost of seed, fertilizer and sprays): feed wheat, 14 per cent; feed barley, 13 per cent; maincrop potatoes, 13 per cent; sugar beet, 14 per cent; oil seed rape, 12 per cent. (These percentages would be much higher if calculated on the gross margins the farmer would expect if he had to sell his crops on the open market without price-support mechanisms or subsidies.) If we look at the use of sprays as a percentage of total inputs – including bought-in feed, fertilizers, sprays, fuel and oil, electricity, heating fuel and so forth – we get a good idea of which farming systems are most extravagant in their use of -cides. Specialist cereal growers come out top with 6·1 per cent (these are 1978/9 figures); followed by general cropping with 5·5 per cent, horticulture with 3·8 per cent, and then the livestock systems, all below 1 per cent.

Kicking the habit

'We don't have any blanket spray programme,' says Horton-Fawkes of Farnley Hall. 'If we don't think we're going to run into bother, we don't spray. On the grasslands we do spray the docks and the thistles, but with a very specific spray. And I often consult people like David Stickland before I spray.'

'I don't condemn everybody who uses fertilizers and sprays,' says Richard Fry down at Rushall. 'But what I do condemn is the total reliance on chemicals. We're proving that you can farm without chemicals and without killing everything in the ground.' Barry Wookey adds that there is no excuse for using chemicals unless you're having a very difficult time with pests and disease.

'If one of my farmers rings up and says he has a disease problem, I tell him to keep an eye on it,' says Stickland. 'If it gets very serious I'll tell him to spray and sell his crop elsewhere. But on the whole the Organic Farmers & Growers members have few problems with pests and disease. Good husbandry keeps them in check.'

But just because the OFG farmers and other low-input and organic men are managing with very little pesticide use, it doesn't mean that other farmers will automatically follow the same route. Indeed the chance of weaning the industry off these chemicals seems slight. Professor Timothy O'Riordan of East Anglia University has emphasised the difficulties – commercial commitments, conservative attitudes amongst users and regulators, and laws that encourage high cosmetic standards in food. There is also the fact that our highly subsidized system distorts the relationship of costs and benefit in a way that favours increased use of pesticides. Professor O'Riordan believes that 'a major effort on a number of fronts will be required if the pattern of pesticide use is to be altered.'

The problem exercised the minds of farmers and experts present at RURAL's first conference in 1983. Integrated pest management (IPM) involves a mixture of biological and chemical control to keep down pest numbers. This has for long been favoured as a good strategy (again, it requires skilled husbandry and observant workers) but the RURAL group which looked at the problem considered another strategy to be both more practical and economically effective: the group favoured a drastic reduction in the use of -cides to an economic threshold 'to minimise the cost of holding a pest down to acceptable levels over the life of the crop without undesirable side effects'. This is what George Cooke was angling at when he called for a thousand-fold reduction. And the RURAL group gave an interesting example of a pest control programme on some Kent fruit farms.

Up to 14 fungal and 5 insecticide sprays are applied to top fruit in the UK in any one growing season. Such a programme is far from cheap. In the 1970s the S.W. Mount farms in Kent decided to reduce spraying in the hope of managing rather than eradicating the pests, the aim being to minimise the cost of holding a pest near its economic threshold during the life of the crop. Coinciding with this effort was the introduction of ultra low volume (ULV) sprayers which produce very fine droplets and better cover of the target area. The volume of pesticide used was reduced from 335 to 55 litres per hectare and allowed the use of insecticides at 10 per cent of manufacturer's recommended rates. In practice this has led to the Mount farms spraying on average 2·4 times a season rather than 4 times as was previously the case, and overall the saving in cost has been considerable. 'There has been an increase in variety of pests seen,' according to the RURAL group, 'but it is reasonable to expect that there will have been a parallel increase in neutral and predatory insects. The Entomological Desert no longer exists.'

We talked to many farmers who either used -cides sparingly (in other words, when the pest or disease had become established rather than as a blanket measure) or not at all. Many said they had from time to time experienced problems, but they considered these minor when compared with what the costs of blanket spray programmes would have been if they'd reacted conventionally. Wookey's men leave cereal fields for ten days or so after harrowing so that the weeds can strike. Then when the field is drilled the mechanical action of the machinery destroys the weed seedlings. In fact his fields looked a lot cleaner than many of the chemically treated fields which one sees full of wild oats and sterile brome. And if you see poppies they will nearly always be in a field where sprays rather than skill is used against the weeds and where the spray has missed.

Sometimes the weed problem in pure organic fields can get too much. 'We have grown spring corn to the OFG 1 standard,' says Horton-Fawkes, 'but we couldn't solve the weed problem. It should have been possible but we could never get onto the fields at the right time to sort them out mechanically.' (Yorkshire weather is not so kind as that in Wiltshire.) 'With the wet springs we're often lucky to get the corn in, let alone leave the fields for ten days before drilling to let the weeds strike.' Nevertheless Horton-Fawkes' spray bill is very modest compared to that of most farmers.

Two researchers who went to study organic farming on the continent both came back to England with similar impressions. On his return Douglas Blair wrote: 'I arrived home from my fellowship quite disappointed in a way because I had expected to discover many different and specialised ways to treat glasshouse pest and disease problems. However there was nothing to discover because there were no serious problems on the holdings visited.' In 1982 Simon Masters visited over thirty research establishments and organic farms in Switzerland, Holland and Germany, and on his return he had little to say about disease and pest control: 'The growers visited did not talk a great deal about pest control other than to point out that a healthy plant rarely suffered from insect or disease attack. In general no greater details were given than this.'

The most comprehensive study so far carried out in this country on the performance of organic farms was done by Anne Vine and David Bateman of the Department of Agricultural Economics at Aberystwyth (*Organic Farming Systems in England and Wales: Practice, Performance and Implications*,

1981). They too had remarkably little to say about the subject of weeds, diseases and pests: 'the organic farmers met do seem to suffer very little from [diseases and pests] and their practices may repay further attention from this point of view.' There are many good reasons why men like Wookey and Horton-Fawkes practise rotational cropping, some of which we discuss in the next chapter, but crop rotation has an important role to play in keeping pests and diseases to a minimum. To follow one crop of wheat with another and another and another is inviting trouble. Wheat and barley should not follow one another as their root systems are similar, and all rotations should be geared to thwarting the spread of diseases. Preventive medicine is what we need.

6 *Moving Mountains*

The views from Witton Fell are stupendous. From the heather
and bilberry which mark the beginning of the moorland, the
valley drops steeply down to the village of East Witton and a
winding belt of trees beyond marks the course of the River Ure.
The grey limestone buildings of Leyburn are perched on the
opposite bank and to the south you can see old pastures giving
way to a patchwork of cereals and temporary leys as the valley
widens out before Masham. On a fine summer's day the horizon
is blurred purple by the North Yorks Moors and the
Hambletons. And just very occasionally, on a fine night, you
can see the petrochemical works burning off gas some seventy
miles away on Teeside. Turn your back on Wensleydale and
you have the moors and hills of the Pennines: thirty miles of
heather, bracken, rough grass, sphagnum bog and wild, almost
uninhabited country; country where the long silences of the
summer months are broken only by the gabbling of grouse, the
searing wail of the curlew and the bleat of Swale and Dales bred
sheep.

Life for the men and women who earn a living in this wild
country isn't easy.

Just below the ridge where Witton Fell meets the moors is
Hammer Farm, 300 acres of marginal hill land down to
permanent grass. It is farmed by Mike and Peta Keeble, two of
the country's best known beef breeders who specialise in
Limousins, a fine breed of French beef cattle. Having spent ten
years managing a 750-acre dairy and arable farm down the
Dales, the Keebles are well aware of the advantages the valley
men have over the hill farmer. 'We've got to cope with colder
weather, more rain, a shorter growing season and the
constraints of poor soils,' says Keeble, who spends some of the
week working away from home while his wife and son manage
the farm. The hill farmer is subject to greater fluctuations in
income than his lowland brothers, reflecting not only the

unpredictability of the climate but the erratic variations of the sheep store market. There is one thing that the uplands can do really well: grow grass. The hill farmer's prosperity must come from beef and sheep.

'The saviour of the hills,' says Keeble, 'must be beef. But the dairy industry dominates the beef market. The milk producers have a dual enterprise. If the hills are to survive, the beef industry must become hill and upland based.'

'Every bullock dies in debt.' The saying is not entirely true but at the moment it is the dairy industry which is taking the lion's share of profitability from beef. Keeble explains: 'A week-old dairy calf today will fetch anything from £40 to £180. Let's say the average price is £120 and the beef rearer will get £450 for the finished animal twelve months later. The gross margin to the producer will then be £330, but 80 per cent of the market price goes on food, labour and so forth. That means we have to deduct £360 from the gross margin. We're left with a debt of £30.' The dairy industry, which supplies over two thirds of all beef animals is therefore doing very nicely, while the beef men struggle. Of course, not all upland beef producers are losing money but the plight of the industry is exemplified by the 40 per cent decline in the beef herd in the Scottish Highlands and Islands over the last decade.

There have been long periods throughout our history when the wild uplands have been viewed with abhorrence by the people of the valleys and the towns, and our present love of these places owes much to the influence of William Wordsworth and the artists and poets of the romantic movement. So great is our love now of the Pennines, of Dartmoor, Exmoor, Snowdonia, the Lake District, the Cairngorms and the peaks of the Western Isles, that many now regard them as our finest landscapes. Great chunks have been designated as national parks and since the last war there has been an increasing tendency for conservationists to think in terms of turning the subsidized farmers of the uplands into glorified park keepers; not overtly, perhaps, but by stealth. It is argued that they should be paid to keep the landscape looking just as it does today, rather than work it productively. Not surprisingly, the hill farmers don't take kindly to this suggestion. 'There must be a way of protecting the uplands without turning them into a vast museum,' says Keeble. And there is. But first we must look briefly at the hill farmers' problems.

About a third of Britain's farming area is classified as upland and most of this is rough grazing land. We can divide the upland systems into two different categories. There are the true mountain farms where there is no low land, and there are the marginal farms which normally have some in-bye or valley land associated with higher ground. The marginal farmer has some distinct advantages over the mountain farmer. The sheep on the mountain farms will generally be purebred hardy animals capable of surviving the harsh climate and poor diet. In Yorkshire it will be the Swaledale; in Wales, the pure-bred Welsh. These breeds will lamb late – in April, May or even June – and the store lambs will be sold in the autumn to be finished off in the lowlands. The marginal farmer will be able to support a flock of half-breds – for example he will cross a mountain sheep with a large down breed ram (a Leicester or a Suffolk, for example) – and he will probably sell his half-bred ewe lambs down to the lowlands where they can be used as breeding stock and fatten up the ram lambs himself. The farmer also has a greater opportunity to grow the silage and hay which he will need to get his sheep and beef cattle through the winter.

Even for the marginal farmer life is far from easy. Barrie Nixon and Martin Turner of Exeter University carried out a financial survey of livestock farms in the south-west between 1977 and 1982 and they found that although gross output on their sample farms increased by 66 per cent over the five years, net farm income actually declined in real terms (total fixed inputs rose by 83 per cent). Profits on cattle and sheep in the south-west, according to the two researchers, 'are insufficient to maintain the necessary investment in livestock, machinery and buildings, as well as a reasonable standard of living.' In the harsher northern climates this situation becomes even worse.

Of course, there is nothing new about this. In many upland areas hill farmers have been struggling for centuries. In many parts of the Pennines the hill farmer's livelihood depended as much on his meagre earnings from the lead mines and the stone quarries as on his agricultural output. When the mines and quarries closed he had to make the land earn a living wage. His inability to do so led to every government since the last war subsidizing upland farming.

Those who farm in what the EEC defines as Less Favoured Areas (LFAs) have been given special assistance, particularly in the form of headage payments (i.e. payment per head of stock) and livestock premiums. The EEC defines maximum levels for Hill Livestock Compensatory Allowances (HLCA), and at the time of writing the UK allowance for a suckler cow is £44.50, for a hill ewe £6.25, and for an upland ewe £4.25. The higher ewe rate is paid for breeds like the Swaledale, the Welsh, the Cheviot and those breeds which the mountain farmer must rely on. A quarter of the costs of these payments are from the coffers of the EEC, the rest coming direct from MAFF. There is a maximum payment of £60 for each hectare.

There are also other schemes wholly funded by the EEC which help the upland farmer. Farmers who earn over half their living from farming and who have no dairy cows are eligible for the suckler cow premium (slightly over £12 a year) regardless of whether or not they are in a Less Favoured Area, and under the EEC sheepmeat regime a Sheep Annual Premium (of around £3) is paid for all female sheep over a year old. At the time of writing there is a 68p supplement for the LFA farmer. The sheep and beef men are also helped by support at the market place. Support for beef producers comes from variable premiums which are calculated to maintain returns at the level of a seasonally adjusted target price. The scheme is underpinned by intervention buying. (Between January 1982 and the end of September 1982, 7,400 tonnes, less than 1 per cent, were sold into intervention.) The maximum for the variable premium (again, for September 1983) is 10.76p per kilogram. The target price today is 108.40p per kilogram. The average market price is 95.94p per kilogram. The EEC will make this up to 106.70, slightly under the target price.

Support for fat sheep is much more spectacular. Under the EEC sheepmeat regime farmers can benefit from the variable sheepmeat premium. The market is supported by variable premiums which are deficiency payments equal to the difference between the average market price in any week and a guide price fixed by the Community. For example, for the last week in July 1983 the guide price was 226.30p per kilogram and the average market price 106.80p. The variable premium was 119.53p, which on a 20 kilogram lamb worked out as £23.90. The farmer therefore gets a slightly larger cheque from the EEC than he does from the auctioneer. The EEC sheepmeat regime has led to a dramatic increase in the number of sheep in this country. As Malcolm MacEwen and Geoffrey Sinclair suggest in their classic 1983 study, *New Life for the Hills*, 'The sheepmeat regime is a typical example of an agricultural policy conceived in isolation, designed to increase farmers' incomes and to generate increased production in excess of demand, without regard to the environmental or social consequences.' Since 1980 the breeding flock has been increasing at the rate of about 3 per cent a year. Wool, incidentally, provides little more than pocket money for most farmers.

The Less Favoured Areas also get rather higher rates of grant than farmers outside these areas. For example, under EEC development plans, drainage works within LFAs are eligible for a 70 per cent grant towards costs whereas outside LFAs the farmer can only claim 50 per cent. For land improvements the LFA man can claim 50 per cent whereas others can only get 32·5 per cent.

MacEwen and Sinclair calculated that agricultural support for LFAs in the UK in 1980 worked out at £131 million, shared between 52,000 farmers. The average support figure for each farmer thus came to £2500. The same two researchers looked at the distribution of headage payments in the LFAs of England and Wales and they found that the 759 largest farmers (3·7 per cent of the total of 20,520 farmers in the LFAs) received 22·4 per cent of the £45 million distributed in 1981-2, or an average £13,192 each. At the bottom of the scale the 11,000 smallest farmers with less than 50 livestock units (1 cow = 1 unit; 1 sheep = 0·15 units) averaged only £590 each.

Government attitudes towards supporting the upland farmer are ambivalent. This country interprets the LFA directive in an extremely unimaginative way, seeing the uplands entirely as food producing areas and favouring the full-time farmer. Yet in 1981 Peter Walker, the then Minister of Agriculture, admitted in the House of Commons that 'The principal objective of the Directive is not to encourage production but to compensate farmers in order to ensure the continuation of farming.' This is a curious admission. The incentives and subsidies have encouraged production; they have not ensured the continuation of farming for large numbers of farmers: between 1950 and 1976 the numbers of holdings in the LFAs fell by 40 per cent.

MacEwen and Sinclair asked a number of rhetorical questions about the fate of the uplands. There has been much support from within farming circles for their conclusions and we can do no better than restate both their questions and answers. We simplify them here.

Q: Has the support system been effective in encouraging food production in LFAs?

A: Unequivocally yes. But there is still scope for increasing food production in the uplands, 'less by capital intensification than by good husbandry, taking more care and using more labour'. There is little or no incentive for small-scale enterprises which could increase local incomes.

Q: How effective is UK policy in the LFAs in ensuring the continuance of farming and thereby stemming rural depopulation?

A: Since the Agriculture Act of 1947, farm amalgamation has accelerated and the agricultural population in the uplands has declined. The researchers point out that the Countryside Commission suggested to the House of Commons Agriculture Committee that 'the Bavarian Government's policy of encouraging part-time farming, instead of being "30-40 years behind us" (as one MAFF official had put it) was in fact a forward-looking and enlightened alternative approach designed to encourage the diversification of rural employment.' MAFF's interpretation of the EEC Directive favours the large, highly capitalised farm employing the minimum of labour.

Q: Does the support system reflect the severity of permanent natural handicaps affecting farmers' activities?

A: No. The UK measures out support as if the LFAs were uniformly handicapped, 'whereas the severity of the handicaps varies enormously'. Sinclair – in a separate upland landscapes study – reached 'the startling conclusion that the support varies inversely with the degree of disadvantage.' This is because farmers on better land can stock it more heavily, thus maximizing headage payments and generating more capital to finance grant-aided improvements. The land can then carry more stock and attract more livestock allowances.

MacEwen and Sinclair found that the support system made little contribution to the resolution of wider social and economic problems and it has done very little to create new jobs. Farmers are going out of business. Those who remain, particularly the smaller ones, cannot afford to maintain either their buildings or the stone walls which control stock movements. Pastures which once yielded good grass are reverting to marsh and bracken. Indeed research at Aberystwyth University suggests that the annual loss of agricultural land to bracken may be as high as 25,600 acres. These great carpets of bracken are of no use to the farmer and are hopeless for wildlife. A fine autumn view is not necessarily a reflection of good land-use. Sheep, which now dominate the uplands, can do nothing to keep bracken in check. Cattle can. There just aren't enough where they are needed.

The farmer who looks down from the heights of Witton Fell towards the Vale of York may feel a twinge of envy, but in fact, for the plains man, the gross margins for fat stock compare so unfavourably with those for cereals that he is unlikely to carry stock at present (although the sheepmeat regime has encouraged some lowland farmers to invest in sheep). He may run a dairy herd, but then there's good money in milk. It may be true that the intensive dairy producers and the high-yield cereal specialists are nearing the end of their artificial prosperity, but today the gulf between lowlands and uplands is as great as it has ever been, and EEC and MAFF policies serve only to deepen it. The salvation of British farming lies partly in future policies breaking down this divide and integrating the arable systems of the lowlands with the stock rearing of the uplands.

The Keeble Plan

Keeble advocates what the continentals call transhumance: large scale shifts of livestock from the summer pastures in the hills onto the lowland plains in winter. It is a wide-ranging plan which could do much more than help the ailing hill farmer. It could help lowland farmers to reduce their nitrogen bill, to use cereal straw which they have been burning, to reinstate cropping patterns which will help to minimise disease, thus reducing the use of -cides, and to utilise more labour more efficiently throughout the year. It will enable the upland farmer to support higher numbers of stock throughout the summer (or to reduce his nitrogen usage) and to cut down on his bills for concentrates and fuel during the winter. If the Keeble Plan was practised on a large scale it could go a long way towards reducing the surpluses of both the dairy and the cereals sectors.

As we pointed out at the beginning of this chapter, the beef and dairy industries are closely integrated. The Keeble Plan will divorce them. He suggests that the dairy industry should be encouraged to dispose of its calves without them entering the beef industry. This effectively means they must go for veal. The Milk Marketing Board would have to provide inducements for all dairy calves to be killed at a maximum of, say, fifteen weeks. Their meat would then not be in competition with the suckler-produced meat which would dominate the beef market.

Just what incentives and penalties should be used to persuade the dairy farmers to move in this direction is a matter for careful discussion. What one can say is that, given the huge degree of subsidization and regulation that exists at present, the government could exert great leverage without having to subject farmers to restrictions greater than they have to accept already. It is not a matter of increasing compulsion, simply of changing the direction of pressure.

Keeble suggests that the plan could be carried out over a period of ten years, with dairy producers selling 90 per cent of their calves to beef production in the first year, 80 per cent in the second year and so forth. After ten years the divorce of beef and dairy industries would be complete. We would suggest, though Keeble doesn't agree with preferential treatment, that the larger dairy producers should have their allowance cut most rapidly and the small man allowed to carry on selling his calves into the beef trade for longer. But that is just a nuance to the plan. Once the Minister of Agriculture has announced that the dairy industry is to concentrate on producing milk rather than selling into the beef industry he can turn to the upland farmer with a very simple message: We are going to lose 70 per cent of our beef supply in ten years time, and it is up to you to make good the shortfall.

The change will come at a time when the dairy industry, in order to increase yields, is switching production from the Fresian to its more productive cousin, the Holstein. The dairy farmers are in practice moving in Keeble's direction by concentrating on a breed which is incapable of producing quick-growing lean beef. This will be the beginning of the end for the Holstein/Fresian x Angus/Hereford steer. The pedigree beef breeds will stage a comeback. There will be a boom in those beef cows such as South Devons, Shorthorns and Simmentals which are comparatively good milkers, and in pure bred Hereford, Charolais and Limousin bulls.

An example will illustrate how this new emphasis on suckler beef production will work. Let us say we have half a dozen farmers in one of Yorkshire's Less Favoured Areas. They may form a cooperative to organize the shift of their stock down to the lowland plains. The farmers will be running a low-input system of beef and sheep ranching, capitalising on their grass and knowing that by shifting nearly all the stock away for the winter months they need devote little land to growing silage or hay. They can graze all their grass throughout the growing season, so that there can be an increase in stocking rates. The only stock which will remain on the hills in winter will be the breeding ewes.

The suckler cows may be spring or autumn calving. Either way, both cows and calves go down to the lowlands for winter. The spring calf will be weaned in the autumn and spend the rest of its life being fattened in the lowlands; the autumn calf will come back up to the hills with its mother, before returning to be fattened up in its second winter on the low ground. Nature dictates lambing time. Sheep will only mate in autumn for spring births (although with modern veterinary techniques it is possible to alter breeding times). Mountain sheep lamb between April and June and the cross-bred sheep on marginal land between February and April. The marginal man can fatten up his own lambs in 14 to 20 weeks (slaughtering at a weight of 40 to 50 pounds) whereas the mountain man will send his store lambs down to the lowlands and they will be slaughtered for the January to March market.

We now have three groups of cattle to be brought down to the lowlands for the winter. There are the suckler cows, all of which must be fed conserved forage or straw-based rations until their return in the spring; autumn calves, which will also return to the hills; and spring calves, which remain on the lowlands to be fattened up.

Naturally the success of the plan depends on lowland farmers agreeing to take stock off the upland men during the winter and agreeing to fatten up the bulls and store lambs for the markets. It may be that the upland farmers will pay the lowland farmer an agreed price to grow the necessary fodder crops, look after the animals and dispose of them, or the lowland farmer may actually become a member of the co-op and thus share in the profits according to the success of the venture.

So what would this mean for the lowland man? One can imagine an arable farmer who presently has his 1,000 acres down to crops like wheat, barley and rape. Under the Keeble Plan he might decide to take 250 acres out of cereals for the market and devote them to sustaining and fattening the stock from the hills. A rough estimate suggests that the 250 acres could support about 750 fat cattle a year. Exactly what the farmer grows will be up to him and the upland farmers. Some of his land will be used to grow silage (grass, maize, oats and tares, for example) and some will be down to fodder crops like rape, kale, rye, cabbage, swedes, mangolds and fodder beet. Instead of burning his straw, as he may well have done in the past, and rather than chopping and incorporating it, which he may consider expensive, the lowland farmer will now be using it all, both as bedding for the stock during the winter and as feed. 'He would be able to get his sucklers through the winter,' suggests Keeble, 'on about a ton and a half of straw with pot ale syrup.' Syrup is a distillery by-product which Keeble is concerned with in his non-farming job. Looking at the effects of the plan in its most parochial terms – for this one farmer we have taken as an example – the shift to upland cooperation will mean the following:

* A reduction in output of cash crops like wheat, barley and rape to 75 per cent of the previous level.
* Utilization of all straw.
* Reduction in requirements of nitrogen and other fertilizer as the farmer now has plentiful supplies of farmyard manure.
* The refound ability to establish crop rotations which will help to minimise disease and pests (and thus the use of -cides) and enable the farmer to retain high fertility with the minimum reliance on artificial fertilizers.

In a wider sense it means that the lowland farmer will be doing his bit to reduce the cereal mountains, will be recycling the waste products, and will have reduced his need for support energy.

What does this mean in terms of meat production? First, and most importantly, we shall put an end to the nonsense of castration. We shall be killing entire bulls rather than steers, as the Italians always have. Sam Meadowcroft, director of

MAFF's Rosemaund Experimental Farm told *Farmers Weekly* in 1981: 'We are throwing away £20 a head by not adapting to bull beef. It is a crazy system where the natural advantage of entire bulls is thrown away by castration and then hormones and implants are used to fill the gap.' There are already many beef farmers who don't use implants but they obviously find themselves at a competitive disadvantage. Once we switch to bull beef rather than steer beef we can quite legitimately insist that hormone implanting is made illegal (as indeed it very nearly was in 1981). This will obviously create some problems as far as fencing is concerned, though it is the dairy bulls, not the beef bulls, that are most apt to turn nasty.

The market must be supplied all the year round. This should be no problem if we have spring and autumn calving herds. Farmers could also be encouraged to fatten bulls up to higher weights, say 750 kilos, rather than to the standard 450 kilos, most popular today. This would make good sense as it is costly to get an animal up to 250 kilos but, providing its genetic constitution is right, it becomes much cheaper to put on lean meat from 450 kilos onwards (and it is lean, not fat, that we want). The combination of autumn and spring calvings together with killing out at various weights between 450 and 750 kilos will ensure constant supplies to the fresh meat market. The butcher will favour the larger animals, as the extra size gives him a greater choice of cuts. The only people who will object are the slaughterhouse men, for two reasons. First, the killing lines of many modern plants are designed for average weights of 450 kilos. Second, it costs the same to kill a 450 kilo bull as a 750 kilo bull. Slaughtering and skinning costs as a percentage of carcass weight will thus be reduced by keeping animals to a greater age.

At present a dairy farmer with 300 cows is making good money on his week-old calves. If one assumes 280 calves a year from the herd, of which 60 will be kept as replacements, the farmer will be realising £22,000 a year if the calves average £100 each. All this will change. In ten years time the farmer won't be selling his calves into the beef industry. The animals will be raised in straw yards (on an adapted veal system) but will be slaughtered young so they will not compete with the beef market. How much the dairy producer will get for the calves remains to be seen. It certainly won't be as simple as it is today:

if the market is related to supply and demand (there must be no intervention buying or support assistance), we can certainly expect to see the dairy farmers' income reduced, but this is something that needs to happen if we are to get the dairy industry down to the size where it will be producing what we need, not a subsidized mountain of dairy produce.

The arable farmer in the Vale of York may look at his gross margins and compare them with what he might get should he agree to enter into some form of cooperative contract with the men from the Dales, and he might think it is better to carry on doing what he does today. But let him consider. The CAP is in tatters.[1] The only way the farmer of the future will survive is by reverting to as near to a closed system as he is able. He must be a mixed farmer. And if we have to move mountains to help him then that is what we must do.

Feedstuffs: the damaging cost

British milk producers will tell anyone who cares to listen that they are the most efficient in the world. They will tell you that over two-thirds of the dairy herd is now in units of over 60 cattle whereas the EEC average herd size is 14 and they will point to the ever-increasing yields. The average annual milk yield for a cow in England or Wales is now 5,292 litres. In Brittany it is 4,633 litres and in Ireland 3,459 litres. What they may not mention is that 94 per cent of the increase in milk yields between 1972 and 1978 was attributable not to better utilization of grass but to extra concentrate feeding. A survey carried out for the Milk Marketing Board (*A Comparison of European Dairying* by S.J. Amies, 1983) concluded that if European milk prices were reduced to world market levels, the high investment, tight stocking and heavy concentrate feeding characteristic of UK dairies would not help the high-input farmer as they do today. Only the southern Irish dairy industry, where emphasis is on producing milk from grass rather than from cereals, would survive intact. One of the problems with the modern cow is that it has been bred to respond to the high-input system. Dr Orskov of the Rowett Institute recently pointed out that if the standard cow was fed on what should be a basic survival diet of straw alone (a diet which would slowly add weight to, say, an Irish Moiled Cow) it would lose weight at the rate of about a pound a day and eventually starve to death.

At RURAL's first meeting in 1983 a group of experts looked at the problems of feeding concentrates to ruminants. They calculated that 41 per cent of the total support energy that goes into ruminant production is used in grass production and conservation (silage, hay and so forth) while 38 per cent is used in the production from concentrate feeds. Grass, however, supplies 73 per cent of the metabolisable energy and concentrates a mere 23 per cent. The conclusion is simple; its implications obvious. Grass has a higher efficiency than cereals. This country should follow the Irish example: cut down on the concentrates; pay more attention to grass.

On the hillside north of Otley Nicholas Horton-Fawkes runs a dairy herd of Ayrshires. The Ayrshire is a hardy cow which suits the low input system he practises. Average yields are around 5,500 litres a cow a year. This compares with a 1982 average yield of 5,602 litres for the 1936 farmers costed by ICI. The ICI farmers used an average of 321 kilograms of nitrogen a hectare; Horton-Fawkes used a maximum of 120. The ICI farmers used an average 1·7 tonnes a cow each year; Horton-Fawkes used 1·3. A closer analysis of the ICI figures shows that the Horton-Fawkes route – intelligent use of grasslands and low concentrate feeding – is the right one. 'This report shows there are many herds recorded in the scheme with relatively modest yields but excellent margins. It also shows that there are many high yielding herds with below average margins.'

'Frightening feed price increases are on the way for livestock producers in the new year,' warned *Farmers Weekly* in September 1983. 'At present,' said Pat Lake of the feed compounders, Bibbys, 'we are mixing soya into our rations which cost £155 a tonne to buy. But we will probably have to buy our new supplies for about £210 a tonne. . . . I cannot see anything at the moment which will prevent a terrific price rise after Christmas.' The poultry and pig sector, where feed represents about two-thirds of costs, will be very hard hit. 'I fear the whole intensive livestock sector could be severely cut back,' said Roger Dean of the UK Agricultural Supply Trade Association.

Getting there: the low-input road

'When I decided we'd stop using artificial fertilizers,' says

Barry Wookey down in Wiltshire, 'I went to see the boss of our seed merchants and I told him I wanted a proper grass mix for organic fields. Then I asked the local vet what trace elements grazing animals required. He told me. The whizz kids from the seed merchants came to see me and they suggested I sow rye grass, timothy, cocksfoot – you know, the normal mix for chemical fields. So I said: "Where do the stock get the manganese, the cobalt, the copper, the iron and all the other trace elements they need?" They went away and returned a month later with a decent mix. "We've never been asked that question before," they said sheepishly.'

Modern grasslands tend to consist of a small number of species which are highly responsive to heavy doses of nitrogen. Wookey's seed mix is much more complicated. It contains rye grass, cocksfoot, white clover, wild white clover, timothy, creeping red fescue, and herbs like burnet, chicory and sheep's parsley. The deep rooting herbs are in the mix because they are very good at accumulating minerals. Clover is important as a nitrogen fixer and its disadvantage of causing bloat is offset by chicory's supposed anti-bloat properties. Cocksfoot is also a deep rooting plant and helps to increase the depth of the soil profile and thus bring nutrients up from deep down, and it helps the sward withstand drought better.

Grass plays an important part in most rotations. Wookey has experimented with different combinations of crops but he has now settled on three years grass, followed by two years corn, the second being undersown with red clover and grazed in the autumn, a hay crop the following summer and then a break for a fallow. Finally he gets another two years of corn before returning to three years of grass. Roots are often fitted into the rotation.

It is the use of legumes and the recycling of organic wastes that ensures that soil fertility is maintained. The inclusion of fodder crops in a rotation helps to clean the ground of arable weeds and acts as a break crop against cereal pests and diseases.

Research by Dr David Thomson of the Grassland Research Institute (GRI) shows how important nitrogen-fixing legumes will become in the future. Thomson has found that dairy cows which graze clover during the first fifteen weeks of lactation can yield 5,900 litres over 305 days without any concentrate feeding. Cows grazing unsupplemented rye grass produce only

5,100 litres. He also found that beef cattle can put on 1·2 kilograms a day on ad-lib fed white clover compared to 0·9 kilograms on grass only. Thomson was reported in *Farming News* as saying that the day may not be far off when home grown legumes meet most of the protein needs of ruminants. This is good news for three reasons: it will cut down feed costs, liberate land now producing feed for other purposes and keep the farmers' fertilizer bill down.

At the GRI at Hurley five bullocks were kept on a one-acre paddock down to a grass/clover sward. The 450 kilogram cattle remained on the sward for three months and gained one kilogram of liveweight a day. No nitrogen fertilizer was used. In another experiment over five years researchers found that mixed grass/clover swards receiving no nitrogen produced 82 per cent of the dry matter of grass swards receiving 320 units per acre of nitrogen. The annual cost of applying the nitrogen was £345 an acre.

There is absolutely no doubt that before too long the nitrogen-fixing plants will have to supplement farmyard manure to keep soil fertility high. In twenty years, at the very most, we shall regard the use of artificial fertilizers as extravagant and anachronistic. It may be that we shall continue to use nitrogen in small doses to get early bite on our grasslands, but the rotation of crops, use of all animal and crop residues and the inclusion of nitrogen fixing plants in grass and fodder crops will serve us well. Some scientists have suggested that we may one day develop strains of cereal that will contain in their roots the nitrogen-fixing bacteria that are at present confined to clover, alfalfa, lucerne, sainfoin and other legumes.

'If your grazing management is right,' says Horton-Fawkes, 'you can dramatically reduce the nitrogen input.' His cows are improving the land year by year. Similarly farmers who have decided to switch from chemical to organic husbandry have found that yields gradually improve as the soil gets into better shape. In their study of organic and semi-organic farming, Anne Vine and David Bateman made the following observation:

> It is often argued that organic farming [using large quantities of locally produced off-farm waste] is not of interest, because there is not enough waste to make it of widespread use. In effect, however, it may be that these farmers are putting

themselves in a very favourable position for the future. Having built up a high level of biological activity and turnover in the soil, it may be that a system with a substantial pasture component will subsequently only need topping up with low inputs of nutrients from outside to keep up the momentum. Many organic farms have been, or are, going through this process of building up a high level of organic matter and biological activity, before becoming comparatively low-input subsequently.

Nobody, including the organic farmers themselves, expects the industry to go entirely organic, although more and more farmers are switching to the organic system and an even greater number will be practising the sorts of husbandry which conform with the Organic Farmers and Growers grade 2 (biological farming topped up with safe chemicals). The organic farmers provide evidence that output need not necessarily plummet with a decrease in chemical inputs. Vine and Bateman found in their survey of seventy organic and semi-organic farmers that cereal yields on organic farms averaged around 90 per cent of standard (with a range of 54 per cent to 114 per cent) for wheat crops grown out of grass, and 90 per cent (range 50 per cent to 122 per cent) for spring barley crops. Stocking rates varied from 32 per cent to 132 per cent of standard with an average for 27 farms of about 80 per cent. Organic farms invariably used less energy per hectare, though their output per £1 of energy is only marginally superior to that of conventional farmers. There is no doubt, however, that we could decrease fertilizer imputs dramatically without suffering great decreases in grass and crop yields.

Livestock producers who rely today on high cereal feed inputs may interpret Cain's slaughter of Abel as a historical precedent for their present plight. Abel was a stockman; Cain an arable farmer. There wasn't much that Abel could have done to stave off disaster, but the modern livestock producers can. They can shift their stock onto a more grass-oriented regime. This, of course, is fine for beef and cattle, but pigs and poultry will still have to be fed on cereal-based feeds. As we have repeatedly stressed, both poultry and pigs fit well into arable rotations provided soil conditions are suitable. And providing they are not in large units the arable man will be able to grow most of his own feed for them.

It is extremely sad that most of the agricultural research carried out in this country is geared towards improving the efficiency of high-input systems of farming. It is vitally important that the Agricultural Research Council turns its attention to developing the breeds and varieties which are suited to low-input systems. It is symptomatic of the malaise in official thinking that the task of conserving rare breeds, whose genetic traits may be of vital importance in future breeding programmes, has fallen to the individual farmers who are members of the Rare Breeds Survival Trust (RBST). When the Trust was founded in the early seventies it was considered distinctly cranky. That is no longer so. It celebrated its tenth anniversary with the opening of a permanent stand at the Royal Showground in 1983. Of the 145 indigenous breeds of cattle in Europe and the Mediterranean region, 115 are in danger of extinction. The importance of the Trust's work will become increasingly apparent as our scientists develop the breeds best suited for the thrifty agriculture of the next century.

7   Wildlife and Landscape: Common Heritage or Private Nuisance?

On a scorching afternoon in mid-July fifty-odd members of the Jethro Tull Club made their way to Kingston Hill Farm near Oxford. Poul Christensen, tenant of the 725-acre mixed farm, led them into a barn behind the farmhouse. We sat on rows of straw bales and listened to Russel Matthews of Cobham Resource Consultants explain why Kingston Hill was one of the Countryside Commission's ten demonstration farms. He pointed out the lie of the land and showed us on a map which parts of the farm we were to visit. Before we left, Christensen said: 'Let me knock this word conservation on the head. All it means is sensible management of the land.'

Ten minutes later two trailers were carting the club members along a track beside a field of maize. There were people from the Agricultural Development Advisory Service, people from the Agricultural Research Council, people from ICI research stations and others from teaching institutes. All the club's members are from the Thames Valley. We could just make out the line of willows where Christensen's land met the river.

Christensen explained why his hedges were important: to keep stock in; for the wildlife; for the view. He showed us a shelter belt he'd planted which was five yards across. The oak, lime and wild cherry which dominated the hedge had been planted four years ago. They were now about ten foot high and full of nesting birds. 'If you've got a hedge,' observed one man rather sourly, 'it means you're paying for it.' He went on to suggest that everything that a farmer does which isn't maximizing profits means he is effectively spending money rather than making it. We rumbled on a hundred yards. Matthews showed us a fine old hedge which once marked the parish boundary. Christensen maintains it by coppicing every fifteen years. The sceptic was unimpressed: 'Why should the farmer pay for industrial archaeology?'

'You should only control weeds if there is an absolute

necessity to do so,' said a man from the Agricultural Research Council's Weed Research Centre. We pointed to a fine tangle of thistles, nettles and mugwort beside the track. 'But the conservationists wouldn't mind if you cleared those away,' we suggested. He gasped at the heresy. 'I disagree,' he said. 'Think of the insects they will be harbouring. Many of them will be beneficial.'

The afternoon wore on and we looked at Christensen's hedge management and a fine block of woodland. 'It is the farmer's responsibility to keep farming operations out of uncropped areas,' said Christensen; adding, almost as an afterthought: 'It seems incredible that we spend so much money on agrochemicals and yet have no idea what effects sprays have on the surrounding countryside.' He'd worked out that on a 25-acre field about 2.5 per cent of the fertilizer used ends up in the hedgeback rather than on the field.

Finally we returned to the barn and slaked our thirst with tea. 'When we came here,' said Christensen before we departed, 'our minimal aim was to make sure that when we leave there will be as many species of plant and animal as there were when we came.' And there will be.

In 1974 the Countryside Commission – the government's landscape and access watchdog – decided to establish a series of demonstration farms to see if it was possible to combine conservation with profitable farming and to find out how conservation could be practised with the greatest ease and least cost for the farmer. The man who got the job of finding the farms and setting up the project was Ralph Cobham. He knows as much as anybody about the business of conservation on the farm. An hour with Cobham and you realise why there are no easy solutions to the conflicts which have now become a perennial feature of British rural politics.

'When we set the project up,' said Cobham as we headed towards 285 acres of ancient woodland on the Bovingdon Hall Estate in rolling Essex, 'we had to decide what sort of audiences we wanted to influence.' This particular day it was a small group of workers from the Farming and Wildlife Advisory Group (FWAG), people already convinced of the conservation case but keen to learn how to help other farmers. 'First, we wanted to provide practical answers for commercial farmers and landowners and we set out to identify the opinion leaders.

81

Then there were the genuine sceptics; the men who say, "We've got to make a living; we can't afford to think about conservation." Then there were the students. We've always considered this one of the most important groups. Our aim has been to catch them and show them how conservation can be integrated into farm management before they go home and "rape" their own farms. We've devoted special attention to explaining the issues and practical results to students and I think we've got through to many of them.'

Cobham stopped to tell the FWAG group about the landowner's willow planting schemes on the farm. Every year John Tabor plants a hundred cricket bat willows along farm ditches and watercourses. And every year he harvests a hundred, making about £40 clear on each.

'Another group we've concentrated on,' continued Cobham, 'are the conservationists themselves. Their knowledge of land use and farm economics is often extremely poor and biased. We've tried to open their eyes to understand the practicalities of commercial farming but one of our biggest problems has been getting through to them.'

Does demonstration work? It has undoubtedly been a success with students although Cobham suggested that college lecturers needed more training. The approach has also helped a number of farmers and landowners who have come specifically to learn about the best tree planting, weed control or hedge cutting methods. And the demonstration projects have worked well with ADAS people: 'We recognised that ADAS more than any other statutory agency has the farmer's ear. They still have much to learn and they are the first to admit it.' In 1978 Sir Nigel Strutt, in his report to government on Agriculture and the Countryside, suggested that ADAS should develop a role as conservation advisors. The government ignored his advice but even had it taken it some years would have passed before the officers would have received the necessary training. One farmer we spoke to suggested it would been an impossible task for ADAS: 'How can ADAS start telling people to conserve, say, ten per cent of their old pastures when it's spent the last twenty years encouraging them to plough them out?'

One thing many of the demonstration farmers have noticed is that conservation techniques they are using are often mimicked by surrounding farmers. Other tenants of St John's College have visited Christensen's farm and returned to their own to plant copses and hedges in a similar way. And the demonstration farm project has undoubtedly shown that conservation doesn't have to cost a lot of money.

Guardians and destroyers

Michael Chandler is the tenant of Hurst Farm down in Dorset. This is no demonstration farm and the management plans are in his head rather than on paper. But Chandler is as eager as anybody in the countryside to conserve the wildlife. He's the chairman of Dorset FWAG and a former chairman of the county branch of the NFU. 'I reckon that about five per cent of Dorset farmers are actively interested in conservation,' says Chandler. 'About ninety per cent don't practise any positive conservation management but they are certainly sympathetic. Then there are the five per cent who will do whatever they believe is necessary to maximise profit.'

These are the black sheep. These are the ones who will be to blame if farmers end up having to apply to local authorities for planning permission before they do anything on their farms.

'In the past the aim was to get ninety-nine per cent of the land into agricultural production,' says Chandler. 'But there is always going to be eight or nine per cent which will never be productive and we must leave this for the wildlife.' This might come in the form of hedges, streams, small copses, large woodlands, rich heathlands: in fact, it could be any of the dozens of habitats that we have in this country. On Chandler's farm there is a magnificent area of scrub beside the River Frome. Salmon spawn under a small bridge and he's hoping that otters will come back to the artificial holt that the Otter Trust has built. The scrub is home to blackcap, chiff chaff, tree creeper and nuthatch. Great-spotted woodpeckers drum away at the trees, and sedge warbler and reed bunting breed in the reeds beside a pair of small ponds. Chandler is frightened that unless the black sheep behave themselves harsh controls will be brought in. Time is running out. Both the Labour and Liberal parties have pledged themselves to introducing planning controls if they are returned to power.

The government's watchdog is the Nature Conservancy Council. One of its jobs is to run nature reserves, some of which it leases from farmers, others of which it owns. Another of its statutory duties is to pick out the finest wildlife sites in the countryside. These are the awkwardly named Sites of Special Scientific Interest (SSSI) and there are over three thousand of them. They are the *crème de la crème* in Britain's landscape: oak woods which have been here since the ice age; sweeping fens under vast skies; massive cliffs with some of the largest breeding seabird colonies in the world; domed bogs where tiny iris grow beside carnivorous sundew plants; and chalk grasslands which supported the enormous flocks of sheep that made the wool industry so important in late medieval times. Some SSSIs are many thousands of acres. Others are less than an acre.

Saving all Britain's SSSIs is simply not enough. 'If the Nature Conservancy saved all the SSSIs,' says Eric Carter, director of FWAG and former deputy-director of ADAS, 'and the rest was left to agricultural development, then we'd just have a tiny percentage of the land surrounded by a sea of. . . . ' He doesn't finish the sentence. There's no need to. 'FWAG's concern,' says Carter, 'is with the eighty-five per cent of the land surface which has no designation to help protect it.'

There has, inevitably perhaps, been a tendency for the leaders of the conservation movement to concentrate their attention, and thus that of the public, on our most special areas: on the magnificent Somerset Levels; on the Broads; on the heaths of Exmoor; and on the fragile peaks of Ben Eighe, Cairngorm, Snowdonia and Helvelyn. But in many ways it is the commonplace in the countryside which is most important. It is the small patch of bluebells in a small oakwood in the undesignated eighty-five per cent. Or a stream which runs by the farmyard with its banks of flag iris and nesting sand martin. Or the couple of acres of wet meadow on the edge of the village with its profusion of ragged robin, purple orchid and marsh hellebore.

The importance of the ordinary and the commonplace in nature is well described by the nineteenth-century essayist William Hazlett:

It is not the beautiful and magnificent alone that we admire in Nature; the most insignificant and rudest objects are often found connected with the strongest emotions; we become attached to the most common and familiar images as to the face of a friend whom we have long known, and from whom we have received many benefits. It is because natural objects have been associated with the sports of our childhood, with air and exercise, with our feelings in solitude, when the mind takes the strongest hold of things, and clings with the fondest interest to whatever strikes its attention; with change of place, the pursuit of new scenes, and thoughts of distant friends; it is because they have surrounded us in almost all situations, in joy and in sorrow, in pleasure and in pain; because they have been one chief source and nourishment of our feelings, and a part of our being, that we love them as we do ourselves.

Nature is thus our universal home and the familiar features of the local farm are as important as the SSSI.

The conflict

In February 1983 some farmers on the Somerset Levels burnt three effigies for the benefit of the media. One was of Sir Ralph Verney, then chairman of the Nature Conservancy Council and a former chairman of the Country Landowners' Association.

The Levels cover almost 170 square miles. Up to the end of the last war low-input grazing was the main activity in this marvellous patchwork of meadowland and marsh. There was no conflict between the farmer and the immensely rich wildlife. By the end of the seventies, however, a high percentage of the Levels had switched to more intensive production. Drainage works helped to upgrade pasture. But there were still a few magnificent areas. In particular there was West Sedgemoor, an area of 2,500 acres. It is criss-crossed with dykes and rhynes, ditches rich in plants. Since 1977 several piecemeal drainage schemes have been grant-aided by the Ministry of Agriculture to 'improve' grazing land. In 1982 the NCC decided it had to declare West Sedgemoor as an SSSI if there was to be any chance of saving it. In fact the NCC had no choice. Under the 1981 Wildlife and Countryside Act it was obliged to designate the area. Hence the burning effigy of Sir Ralph. There were bitter disputes between conservationists and farmers, both in the press and on the ground. A few weeks later Sir Ralph was informed that his contract would not be renewed.

The Sedgemoor saga is not the only major conflict we have

seen between farmers and conservationists over the last decades, but it provides us with a good insight into why the tension has arisen. So much has been written on the subject of conflict that we shall deal with it briefly and get back to the business of how conservation can become an integrated part of all farm management. As indeed it must.

Britain's wildlife and landscape has taken a severe battering since the last war. The farmer has been encouraged to drain marshes, to fell deciduous woodlands and to rip out hedges, often with large subsidies from the government. Farmers have been encouraged to bring marginal lands, like the grazing meadows of the Somerset Levels and the heaths of Exmoor, into intensive production, and to turn pristine habitats like saltmarsh and woodland into arable land.

A few figures will show the extent of the changes in the countryside. Between 1945 and 1970, 140,000 miles of hedgerow were pulled up. Hedgerow losses still continue though grant-aid for their removal is no longer available. In south-east Scotland 88 per cent of the lowland heaths were destroyed between 1960 and 1980. Between 1937 and 1971 nearly half of Wiltshire's chalk grassland was ploughed up to grow corn. Nearly half of Britain's ancient woodlands, arguably our most precious habitat, has been lost since 1947, more than was lost in the previous four hundred years. And whilst the woodlands have been coming down – some to be converted to coniferous plantations, others to join the stock of arable land – we have been steadily nibbling away at salt marshes, wet meadows and river banks. As Oliver Walston wrote in *Farmers Weekly*:

> The facts are there for anyone to see. Trees and hedges have been pulled out all over the country and this was mainly done by farmers. No matter how many trees we now plant – and we have been planting a lot in recent years – we cannot alter history. Likewise it is a fact that more and more species of wildlife are becoming endangered due to modern farming methods. These facts alone have made the public very unhappy indeed and we are deluding only ourselves if we do not accept this.

The conservationists' arguments are clear. They insist that farmers do not continue to destroy what is so dear to so many when the only benefits which result from intensification accrue to them. Each year, according to the Royal Society for the Protection of Birds, the public foots a £150 million bill for draining wetlands. With surpluses at the level they are, it cannot be argued that it is in the economic interest of the country to have wetlands producing more of what we already have in too great a quantity. In fact the opposite holds true, for it is the tax-payer who must foot the bill to stockpile the surpluses and dispose of them.

The conservationist will point out, again with good reason, that the farmer is in many ways very privileged. He pays no rates. He is not bound by the planning restrictions which mean that anybody else must apply for permission even to add a garage to his house. He has been nobly supported by the government since the last war.

The public is now well versed in the arguments and it is clear that the expansionist farmers are losing sympathy. The farmers' unions have done little to help matters. Take, for example, the following paragraph from *Farmers' Weekly* (August 1983): 'Grants and subsidy payments, without which it would be impossible to efficiently farm less favoured areas, must not become dependent on environmental considerations, the union says.' The union was the Farmers' Union of Wales. This statement is remarkable for two reasons. First, farming cannot, by definition, be said to be efficient if its continuance depends on the farmers receiving a steady flow of public finance. Second, the funding comes from tax-payers' pockets. It would seem reasonable that the tax-payer should have some say in how it should be spent on the farm. Banks, after all, do not lend farmers money unless they have established that it will be used in a particular way. The Farmers' Union of Wales is not only being extremely ungrateful: it appears to ignore the fact that most tax-payers are deeply concerned about the fate of the countryside.

The acrimony which met the NCC's designation of West Sedgemoor was always on the cards. One monolithic government agency, the Ministry of Agriculture, with its vast funds and huge influence, has spent forty years telling farmers to think big. Another, the minute and under-financed Nature Conservancy, was asking farmers to do otherwise. (The NCC, it must be conceded, has never been noted for its expertise in public relations and most of its officers are scientists ill-versed in the ways of the farming world.) Under the Wildlife and Countryside Act the government is obliged to pay handsome compensation to farmers who are asked to farm their land benignly (in the case of the Somerset Levels, to graze it on an extensive basis). It would have been much better had the men at West Sedgemoor accepted the NCC's decision (and money).

It is sad that even designation as an SSSI does not necessarily mean that the site will be safeguarded. David Goode and Angela King carried out a survey of habitat losses for the NCC. They released their results in 1980 and even the NCC seemed shocked to learn that twelve per cent of all SSSIs were being damaged or destroyed each year. In the twelve months prior to the publication of the survey a third of Dorset's SSSI land had been damaged or destroyed. Though organizations like MAFF, its Scottish counterpart, the Department of Agriculture and Fisheries for Scotland (DAFS) and the NFU continued to claim that there was nothing to worry about, other farmers began to speak up. 'Sites of Special Scientific Interest should be welcomed and respected rather than being considered hostile intrusions,' wrote Walston in *Farmers Weekly*. 'All signs telling the public to "keep out" should be removed immediately and replaced with notices welcoming the public – but on our clear terms. They must not damage the crops, endanger the livestock or harm game. If they do, we should tell them to go without hesitation.'

When we began work on this book we drew up a list of conservation-minded farmers to go and see. Nearly every one asked the same two questions: 'You are going to be positive, aren't you? Or is this going to be yet another attack on the farmers?' And each time the answers were yes and no, in that order. We have had no choice but to state the gravity of the present situation. And like the farmers we talked to, we would like the farmers themselves to put their own house in order.

The Farming and Wildlife Advisory Group

A few miles north-east of Blandford Forum, on the heavy Dorset clay, lies the village of Hammoon. It is almost too perfect: the church with its sombre yews, the manor house, the River Stour fringed by willow and reed, the cattle gently chewing the cud in lush grass. It is the pastoral idyll and if you bumped into Constable with his easel you wouldn't be surprised. Mrs Angela Hughes runs East Farm, which is now one of the most intensively studied (and beautifully farmed) pieces of land in Britain. She has managed to show how commercial farming can take place alongside the conservation of wildlife and landscape. And to prove it she has opened her account books at the two conferences which studied East Farm, one in 1970, the other ten years later.

Mrs Hughes manages the 400 acre dairy farm with the help of five men. The whole farm is down to grassland and supports a couple of hundred Fresian milk cows. All the slurry is returned to the fields. The farm is a highly profitable business.

The farm is immensely rich in wildlife. Every pasture is hemmed in by fine hedges and there are nine ponds, all fringed by alder, willow and other trees. There is a disused railway line, now used as a farm track, whose banks are strewn with wild flowers. And there are small woods, copses and spinneys. The list of birds and animals seen on the farm is remarkably similar to what one would expect on a small nature reserve. There are badger, fox, weasel and stoat, three species of shrew and six species of bat. An attempt is being made to entice otters back with an artifical holt, and roe deer are found on the farm. Among the sixty species of bird breeding on the farm are the three British species of woodpecker, though the lesser-spotted is a rare and infrequent breeder. Six species of tit, heron, sparrow hawk, nuthatch, tree creeper, nine species of warbler, spotted flycatcher and cuckoo also breed at Hammoon. The lists of flowering plants and lichens and mosses are equally daunting.

Mrs Hughes knows exactly how to manage all the unproductive bits of her farm. She knows when to cut back the hedges, when to pollard the trees (she has two of the very few black poplars remaining in this country), and when to clear floating vegetation off the top of her ponds. She knows what species to plant when she is establishing new spinneys and copses. She is a very competent naturalist; but there are also a lot of farmers who want to maintain the wildlife habitats on their farms and possibly to improve them who don't have Mrs Hughes' knowledge or expertise. They must seek help from the Farming and Wildlife Advisory Group (FWAG).

'You don't think FWAG's a whitewash, do you?' asked one FWAG county chairman. His concern was genuine. 'At one time I thought it might be,' he continued. 'I didn't want to be involved in a whitewash. I love conservation, you see.' His county group certainly isn't a whitewash.

The seeds of FWAG were sown at a conference at Silsoe in 1969. The Silsoe exercise was organized by a bunch of farming and conservation groups to establish the common ground between them. The National Farmers' Union, the Country Landowners' Association, the Nature Conservancy Council, the Royal Society for the Protection of Birds (RSPB), the British Trust for Ornithology and the Ministry of Agriculture got together on one of the *Farmers' Weekly* farms at Tring in Hertfordshire and worked out ways in which commercial farming could be integrated with conservation. In 1970, largely as a result of the Silsoe exercise, the FWAG was formed and the groups involved at Silsoe have provided representatives on FWAG ever since. The RSPB put up some money and provided space for FWAG's one full time worker in its rural offices outside Sandy in Bedfordshire.

FWAG's history through the seventies was, as far as the conservationists were concerned, fairly uneventful. Many accused it of being a farmers' whitewash. While great areas of marsh were being drained and while woods were going under the chain saw across the country, FWAG devotees were accused of trying to provide a cover up by planting small copses in field corners and doing a little bit of hedge management. But despite the criticisms – and they had some foundation – FWAG was establishing county groups throughout the country. By summer 1983 there were fifty groups and in the last three years FWAG surprised many of its critics by becoming not only influential among farmers but by stating the conservation case in much more uncompromising terms.

The man who runs FWAG is Eric Carter, once in the Ministry of Agriculture, and a man with a deep knowledge both of the farmers' problems and of those of our declining wildlife. He is a deceptively mild man: tall, and thin as a heron, with a kindly demeanour. He is also a diplomat, as indeed are the chairmen of the county branches. The FWAG, both locally and nationally, never gives any opinions on specific issues and thus has a very low profile as far as the media and the public are concerned. Also it never approaches farmers directly. It waits to be approached. It works on the principal that the NCC will look after SSSIs (or try to) and thus concentrates its attention on advising farmers how to look after the more ordinary and commonplace. Any farmer who wants advice on conservation matters can approach FWAG and one of the FWAG advisors will visit him and help him to plan a programme of action. Some county FWAGs remain small and fairly uninfluential. Others, particularly the longest established, are well known in their areas and very active. By 1984 there will be at least five counties with full time advisors. 'We hope to have full time advisors in every county before too long,' says Carter. Suffolk is one of the most progressive groups and the county FWAG has set up a consultancy service. For £15 a year a farmer can get a visit and advice from the group as well as all the literature that FWAG produces.

In April 1983 the Farming and Wildlife Trust Ltd was formed and Wilf Dawson, formerly a leading light with the Society for the Promotion of Nature Conservation (the umbrella body for the county naturalists' trusts), was appointed as director. The Trust has been formed to raise money to support the work of FWAG, and particularly the establishment of full-time advisory posts in the counties. These advisory posts are also going to be grant-aided by the Countryside Commission and the Nature Conservancy Council. The Trust is initially trying to lay its hands on £500,000.

Every farmer can do something for the landscape and for wildlife, and if he needs help he can contact FWAG. However, official policies and price-support systems often encourage farmers to make short-term changes which can be disastrous to wildlife.

However successful FWAG becomes on the ground, and however influential farmers like Angela Hughes and Michael Chandler may be, there will still be the small number of black sheep wrecking their land. And until we get reforms, there will still be government policies encouraging them towards destruction.

Public money: where should it go?

Agricultural intensification, whose justification was enshrined

91

in the 1947 Agriculture Act, made a lot of sense and it did revitalise the industry. Today, however, as we have already suggested, the expansive attitude which was so necessary then is very out of place.

In 1983 there was a public inquiry over whether agricultural reclamation of the Wash marshlands should be banned. The county council favoured the ban. Huge tracts of saltmarsh have already been drained and transformed into high quality agricultural land (grade 1 in the Ministry's classification scheme). Since the sixteenth century 79,000 acres of the Wash estuary have been reclaimed and what is left in the form of mudflats and salt marsh is specially important now. Farming organisations were strongly opposed to the ban and Mr John Kerr of the Country Landowners' Association told the inquiry inspector: 'Reclaimed land from the Lincolnshire coast is of the highest quality. It makes a substantial contribution to food supplies and the national economy.' He was absolutely right, though not in the sense he intended. Increasing the stock of land which produces cereals does make a substantial contribution to food supplies: it swells the surpluses. And it does make a substantial contribution to the national economy, in two ways: it absorbs resources in the shape of grant-aid for the drainage scheme; and it places a further financial burden on the CAP, as the surpluses must be stored and dumped with export refunds. When it is considering grant-aiding projects, the Ministry of Agriculture bases its financial assessments of the schemes on the value of increased production. Its calculations severely exaggerate the economic gains as they make no allowance for the heavy subsidization through support prices. If, for example, the land was to be assessed as a potential wheat-yielding area, the value of the wheat would be calculated at £120 a tonne. This ignores the fact that the price is artificially maintained at around forty per cent above world market prices.

The Severn Trent water authority wants to spend £7 million to widen and deepen twenty miles of the River Soar. The work will be paid for, if it goes ahead, by central government and Leicester tax-payers, through a levy on the county council. The scheme will enable 6670 acres of pastureland to be converted to arable, thus, according to the Authority, bringing £5.8 million worth of benefits to agriculture. Leeds University economists John Bowers and Cyril Black – two men who have done much to highlight the spurious cost-benefit analyses used by water authorities and MAFF to justify drainage schemes – worked out that the Authority had over-estimated the agricultural benefits by £2-2.5 million. The Authority had included government subsidies in the scheme's benefits but excluded them from the costs. It had also made over-optimistic assumptions about crop yields and flood risks.

The Wash and Soar schemes are not isolated examples. Similar poor economics have been used to justify – or try to justify – reclamation and upgrading of land in the Somerset Levels, in Amberley Wildbrooks (where a public inquiry uncovered the Ministry of Agriculture's spurious cost-benefit analysis), on the North Kent Marshes and many places elsewhere. While government encourages farmers through its expansionist policies and grant-aid schemes to continue bringing marginal lands into production (and one of Michael Joplin's first public utterances when he became Minister was that he wanted to encourage increased output) it is not suprising that wildlife habitats continue to be destroyed at an alarming rate. There is little that FWAG or even the Nature Conservancy Council can do to stop the destruction.

What we urgently require is a restructuring of the entire grant-aid system to ensure that ecological and social considerations are taken into account in every development which is publicly funded. It goes without saying that the more benign forms of farming which we are championing – with a dramatic decrease in the use of artificial fertilizers and pesticides; a return to mixed farming and the more extensive grazing of grasslands; a reduction in the amount of land down to cereals which are to be fed to livestock – all this will defuse much of the conflict we now have between commercial agriculture and the conservation of nature and landscape. Nevertheless government policy will remain extremely important, and we must take a look at an alternative package of agricultural subsidies devised by Clive Potter.

Potter is an environmental scientist at East Anglia University. His alternative package of agricultural subsidies (APAS) is a comprehensive attempt to devise a grant-aiding system that will be good for farmers, will be fair in the way funds are distributed, and will encourage farmers to think of conservation as an integral part of farm management. He has adopted a similar approach to the problems of the uplands as did Malcolm MacEwen and Geoffrey Sinclair and he has followed their plans for reforming the headage payment system. Let us look briefly at Potter's suggestions. We do not necessarily endorse all the details (and we certainly do not accept Potter's assumption that we shall continue to have the same levels of price support 'in the context of continued EEC membership') but his work does show how reform of the grant-aid system can play a vital role in conserving the countryside.

Potter has identified three different target groups of farmers in the countryside: farmers in less favoured areas; farmers who have land with special conservation features such as SSSIs; and farmers who work good land of reasonable quality in areas which don't fit into the first two categories. Potter suggests that in the LFAs there should be a redesigned headage payment scheme which will reward less favoured farmers rather than those who farm in such a way as to capitalise most effectively on available subsidies and support mechanisms. Farms with valuable habitats should be eligible for 'special area' grants aimed at protecting their income while fulfilling conservation objectives. Finally, there should be a strong effort to bring conservation management and investment into farm decision-making on the more intensively farmed land.

Farmers who contemplate some form of capital investment at present can apply to MAFF for grant aid under one of two schemes. First, there is the Agriculture and Horticulture Grant Scheme (AHGS). A wide range of developments fall under this scheme: water supply, field drainage, grassland reseeding, land reclamation, fencing and so forth. Only farmers providing enough work to occupy a skilled worker for at least 1,800 hours a year are eligible. About £73 million was spent on AHGS in 1980/81, and £28.3 million of that was on drainage. Second, there is the Agriculture and Horticulture Development Scheme (AHDS) which, rather than chanelling aid into a named capital item, attempts to give assistance within the context of an overall farm development plan. Its main purpose is to help raise poorer farmers' incomes. In 1980 £79 million was spent under AHDS.

Potter has a number of criticisms of the ways in which AHGS and AHDS money is dispensed:
* The smaller farmers benefit the least. They will adopt the most modest schemes as they will have less money available to

match the grant aid (farmers pay a certain proportion of capital cost, varying according to the nature of the development and whether they are in a Less Favoured Area). Bowers has pointed out that with arterial drainage there is a tendency for investment to snowball with an initial scheme giving rise to further schemes eligible for grant aid.

* The plight of the small farmer, whose ability to get grant aid is limited or non-existent, is further aggravated by indirect subsidies such as price support under CAP.

* Both schemes ignore the environmental and social costs associated with many developments.

Potter's APAS for intensively farmed land involves the imposition of a ceiling on the size of investment projects eligible for grant aid. He puts a ceiling at £10,000 (as opposed to the present £136,000 for the AHDS and £100,000 for the AHGS). Second, Potter advocates an increase in the number of conditions attached to grant payment together with a relaxation of conditions of entry to a more wide-ranging version of the AHDS. Conservation vetting should be built into the system and the accent must be on encouraging a larger number of smaller schemes bringing about incremental improvements, rather than funding a limited number of large one-off capital projects. Potter rightly insists that farmers will need to get approval for grant aid before beginning works (an extremely sensible system which prevailed before cost-cutter Lord Rayner advocated abolishing the need for prior approval). Potter calculates that £2 million would be saved as a result of the grant size limit and a further £6.5 million through withdrawal of grant on ecologically damaging schemes. However, about £9.9 million would be required as additional spending, £3.9 as a compensation component of the AHDS, the rest as an AHGS supplementary grant.

Potter then turns his attention to the 'special assistance areas' where it is essential for conservation that traditional farming practices are maintained. These areas would include such jewels as the Somerset Levels, Halvergate Marshes and Exmoor. Potter calculates that £10 million could be saved on compensation and a further £20 million on withdrawal of direct grant aid. However this would be offset by grant aid to special assistance areas worth £21.5 million, and lowland livestock compensatory allowances (for example to retain pastoral grazing on the Levels) worth another £6 million.

Finally, we come to the Less Favoured Areas where Potter sees a saving of £9 million through the restructuring of the headage payment scheme. This will be offset by an additional £9 million spent on an expanded AHDS. Savings under Potter's schemes would total £47.5 million; extra expenditure would total £46.4 million. If APAS were put into operation it would undoubtedly help to conserve much that is threatened through MAFF's thoughtless grant-aid policies. And it would help the small farmer, who presently can benefit little from a system of subsidization and funding which is biased in favour of the man who is highly capitalized.

Many of the lowland habitats which are under the greatest threat today are those where pastoral grazing has persisted for centuries: on the Somerset Levels, on the Norfolk Broads, on the fringes of our estuaries and on coastal salt marshes, and along the flood plains of rivers like the Soar and the Severn. Ignoring all ecological considerations, it would be madness to finance the transformation of these areas from pastoralism to either field cropping or intensive grassland. There the low input systems are best suited to survive the coming years: to switch to arable production is courting disaster. Arable men will be trying to come off the chemical and high-input treadmill over the next decades. The last thing we should do is encourage others to take their place.

However, we certainly are not advocating that land reclamation should cease. There are many areas which are hopeless for wildlife and very poor for the farmer. Particularly in the uplands there are great tracts of in-bye invaded by hard rush and scrub. In the Outer Hebrides an EEC funded Integrated Development Plan threatens to destroy the marvellous machairs (great stretches of floristically rich grassland on shell sand by the sea) while ignoring the most obvious problem: the gradual decline in the quality of the in-bye land. It is in the latter areas that reclamation should take place. And vital to our plan to revive the uplands will be a massive programme to rid the hills of bracken.

For every hundred acres in the British Isles there are three covered by bracken. Once bracken spreads into an area it tends to suppress the growth of other plants and eventually forms a thick monocultural blanket in which neither stock nor wildlife have any real place. According to Jim Taylor, a researcher at Aberystwyth University, the area covered by bracken is increasing at the rate of about 25,600 acres a year. This is a disastrous situation, partly caused by marginal land going out of cultivation between 1920 and 1940 and partly by the tendency of farmers to concentrate on intensive grassland management on lower land and allow the steeper, higher fields to become under-grazed. Sheep, which came to predominate areas now infested by bracken, are less effective at keeping the weed in check than cattle.

'The eventual returns to farmer and nation from bracken clearance,' wrote Taylor in *Farmers Weekly* in 1983, 'would far outpace parallel schemes for improvement of windswept, peaty, open moorlands, which are soon negated by the upland climate, and land drainage of valley land which is expensive to establish and maintain.' According to Taylor, up to a third of Britain's bracken land could be reclaimed without any major conservational risk. The farmer would be able to increase his stocking rates and thus his income.

If we take Taylor's suggestion that a third could be reclaimed without any detriment to conservation (and we believe that this is a gross under-estimate) we could bring back into productive use 27,000 square miles. The cost of eradication by spraying with Asulam combined with either liming and slagging or the use of phosphate and cobalt together with fencing is between £94 and £210 an acre. Compare this with the cost of the Severn Trent scheme to turn 6670 acres from grazing into arable land: a staggering £6420 per acre. It is madness to think of reclaiming areas of great ecological and landscape value in the already heavily farmed lowlands when there is such opportunity for reclaiming, at such modest cost, the degrading bracken lands of the uplands.

To sum all this up, what we need is a reform of the grant-aid system which will make conservation an integral part of farm development. This will be part of the de-escalation programme which we discuss in the final chapter.

But whatever we do to the AHDS and the AHGS there will still be farmers who continue to take not the slightest notice of conservation; and there will be that small number of landowners who claim that they intend to develop an SSSI simply to extract compensation in return for desisting. These are two distinct, though grave problems which we have to face.

In 1981 the government introduced a Wildlife and Countryside Bill. Its passage through the Lords and the Commons was very stormy and it attracted a record 2,300 amendments. There are three sections to the Act. The first deals with the protection of individual species, the second with protection of habitats, and the third with access to the countryside. One of the principles enshrined in the Act is that owners of SSSIs can get compensation for not developing. They can also get compensation if MAFF grant-aid is withheld because the proposed development falls within an SSSI. Another principle which pervades the entire Act is that of trust: trust that conflicts can be resolved by voluntary agreement; trust that landowners will respect their custodial role. This is all very fine, but it means that while responsible owners of SSSIs get nothing for their willingness to look after valuable habitats, all a landowner needs to do to cash in on the compensation bonanza is to threaten destruction. One big landowner, for example, declared his intention to afforest a famous peat bog and received a once-and-for-all payment of around £300,000 for agreeing not to do so. A Hampshire farmer we talked to pointed to the estate of an MP in a neighbouring county. 'It's not a very good example when a man like that gets a six-figure sum for not converting an ancient woodland into conifers, is it?' he said. No, it isn't. What the Act has really done is to establish the NCC as an alternative funding source to MAFF. If anything it has fuelled conflict and encouraged greed. NCC simply does not have the money to protect SSSIs through compensation, especially if it comes in the form of annual payments based on calculations of loss of profit. One Kent farmer has been awarded £100,000 a year not to turn 1,800 acres of grazing marsh on the Isle of Sheppey into arable land. He told the *Farmers Weekly*, 'Had we been able to develop the farm as a cereal unit we would have produced about £600,000-worth of wheat a year and in our area that would have gone for export. The nation is foregoing that money on the balance of payments.' This farmer, like the Severn Trent water authority, has ignored both the EEC's problem of surplus production (for 1983 about 16 million of the 54 million tonnes of wheat produced in the EEC was surplus to Community needs) and the artificially high prices cereals fetch.

In our final chapter we insist that there must be compensatory payments to farmers who are conserving the countryside if they need help, but they must be discretionary. It is scandalous that the public should be expected to donate large sums of money to men who can well manage without.

It is also clearly ridiculous that the impoverished Nature Conservancy Council should be expected to fork out the compensatory grants. The responsibility for doing so must be shifted to the Ministry of Agriculture.

Control: keeping it local

1986 is the ninth centenary of the writing of the Domesday Book, the first and to date the last comprehensive survey of British land and landownership. We must celebrate this great event by repeating the exercise. A latter-day Domesday Book will enable the County Agricultural Committees, on whom we intend to devolve many of the responsibilities cumbersomely performed by MAFF today, to ensure that the black sheep are brought into line. We shall have farmers, with the help of members of the Nature Conservancy, the Countryside Commission and the county councils, ensuring that the magnificent British countryside survives. They are in a much better position to do so than planners who often know little about the countryside and who will attract scant sympathy from the farming community. These County Committees will bear the brunt of the responsibility for carrying through our ten-year programme of de-escalation and they are therefore dealt with more fully in Chapter 9. As far as the conservation aspects of the programme are concerned this won't be too difficult. After all, as Poul Christensen of Kingston Hill Farm said, all conservation means is the sensible management of the land.

8 *Land, Labour and Accountancy*

'So long as the price of land remains so ludicrously high,' one tenant farmer told us, 'you will have farmers exploiting their animals and their soil.' High land prices mean high rents for tenants; they mean high insurance bills for occupiers; they mean colossal Capital Transfer Tax payments for owners.

'So what would you do?' we asked the tenant. 'Get the Tories to nationalize it! If Labour nationalized land it would be seen, quite rightly, as a political move. But if the Tories nationalized it everyone would realize it was because it's the only way to deal with the awful problems of high land prices.'

The relationship between land, labour and capital has exercised the mind of every great economist since time immemorial. We don't pretend to be economists so there will be no great theoretical tract here; but one doesn't need to be an economic wizard to see that there are urgent problems associated with high land prices, a diminishing labour force, the loss of small family farms and the decline of rural communities. We can look at these issues and suggest how the social decline of the countryside can be arrested. Many of these problems are the direct consequence of government and EEC policies.

The problem of decline

'At the end of the war there were nearly one million agricultural workers in the United Kingdom,' said Peter Walker in February 1983. 'In the post-war period there has been a dramatic reduction of two-thirds of that labour force. . . . The reduction in the labour force has been as staggering as the increase in productivity.' In 1982 (according to MAFF's provisional figures) agriculture provided work for just over 700,000 people. Of these, 203,000 were full-time farmers and 92,000 were part-time farmers (farmers being either owner-occupiers or tenants). In addition 171,000 people worked full-time on farms, and 62,000 part-time. Just under a 100,000 people found casual or seasonal work on farms. A further 74,000 wives or husbands of farmers, partners and directors were engaged in farm work. The agricultural labour force represents 2·8 per cent of the total civilian workforce. Greece has 30 per cent of its labour force on the land, Ireland 19 per cent, Italy 13 per cent, France 8 per cent and Germany 6 per cent.

The land labour force in Britain declined particularly rapidly during the 1970s at an annual rate of around 4 per cent. It has slowed slightly in recent years but the decline is still at a significantly high annual rate of 2 per cent. Government policies, as we have shown, have continually favoured the reduction of labour on our farms and there have been no positive efforts to encourage farmers to retain labour. In fact labour has been about the only thing which has not at some time been subsidized.

The decline in the labour force has been particularly severe in the uplands. For example between 1965 and 1973, 79 per cent of the full-time labour force in Snowdonia disappeared as farms became more mechanized. MacEwan and Sinclair have pointed out that although 90 per cent of the land in the uplands is used for agriculture, the industry only provides one in five jobs. Forestry has proved an even worse employer. A report issued by the Country Landowners' Association in 1980 pointed to modern agriculture's poor labour potential: 'One of the main difficulties facing the Common Agricultural Policy has been that it has tried to solve the social problems of rural areas by subsidizing the incomes of farmers in these areas. The provision of alternative employment in rural areas could well be a much better way of dealing with this problem.' We return to the CLA's advice in a few pages.

The drift of labour from farms into our cities – where increasingly the worker finds unemployment rather than better pay in industrial jobs – is only one facet of the social decline in the countryside. The nature of our farms has dramatically changed over the past century. Farms have become larger and fewer. There has been a striking rate of decline in the number of farms: over 16 per cent in England in the decade up to 1982; slightly less in Wales. Taking England and Wales together, the losses amounted to 40 per cent of holdings under 2 hectares, 23 per cent of holdings between 2 and 20 hectares, 15 per cent of holdings between 20 and 40 hectares and 5 per cent of holdings between 40 and 200 hectares. In particular counties the losses were even greater: in Bedfordshire, for example, 47 per cent of holdings under 2 hectares were lost, and in Norfolk 31 per cent of those between 2 and 20. Meanwhile, during the same ten years, the percentage of land in holdings over 200 hectares rose from 31 per cent to 36 per cent for all England and Wales and in Norfolk from 49 per cent to 54 per cent. These are staggering figures and they reflect the Community's policy of encouraging farm amalgamation. As Hew Watt, an Essex farmer, pointed out in *Farmers Weekly* in 1983, the CAP's Modernisation of Farms Directive (72/159) 'has long since served its purpose and is now creating more problems than it solves'.

In the 1970s there was a huge upsurge in land buying by financial institutions. To bring up the subject with many farmers is like waving a red rag at a bull. The institutions have been blamed for many things, some justifiably, others unreasonably. Surveys by Savills and Roger Tym & Partners showed that during the late seventies institutions were acquiring land at the rate of about 50,000 acres a year. At the end of 1981 financial institutions owned about 685,000 acres. Over half the land owned by the end of 1981 had been bought since 1976, and their ownership is concentrated on higher quality grade 1 and grade 2 land, particularly in the east Midlands and East Anglia. Recent figures from Savills suggest that institutions are losing interest in land acquisition. They can see that changes in CAP are likely to come about which will decrease the profitability of farming. Also, land has not appreciated as much as many were hoping, and land bought with borrowed money can no longer be counted such a good investment as inflation has now fallen far below bank borrowing rates. However, one of the reasons why institutional buyers bought less in 1982 than in any other year since 1976 was that very little top grade land came onto the market.

So, briefly, what can we hold against the man from the Pru? First, the institutions have been accused of being interested only in squeezing profit out of the land as fast as possible, and conservationists have noted the alarming way in which many institutions have cleared woodlands, hedges and marshes from their land. Second, the institutions have been accused of pushing up land prices. With their large capital backing they have been in a position to bid unrealistically high prices for high class land, thus exacerbating the problem of high land prices. Both of these criticisms have some validity. However to make too much of the institutions' appearance on the land market is to ignore the problems caused by farmers themselves. According to Professor Michael Haines of Aberystwyth University, 80 per cent of the land which changed hands in Britain in the 1970s was absorbed by farmers enlarging their existing holdings. 'These farmers,' says the professor, 'can generally afford to pay a higher price for the land than other prospective buyers precisely because they may not need to invest in other fixed resources to exploit it.'

In an article in *Farmers Weekly* in 1983 Norman Coward of the Midland Bank insisted that farmers are now the main determinants of land values in the UK: 'The City has not been buying as vigorously in the last few years and rarely does it now buy vacant possession land – it does not, therefore, compete with farmers in that market.'

It has been the small and part-time farmer who has suffered most since the last war, for reasons which we have already discussed or hinted at. In the Less Favoured Areas it is the larger man who has been best able to capitalize on government grants, and the same is true in the lowlands. 'The Midland Bank – the listening bank – listens only to the big farmers,' a Huddersfield farmer complained to *Farmers Weekly*. And while the banks listen to the big men, the Ministry of Agriculture discriminates in its grant-aiding schemes against the small men and the part-timers. For most schemes only farm units capable of supporting a full-time worker for more than 1,800 hours a year are eligible. Part-time farming is very important in many European countries but it is officially scorned here. 'The full-time farmer is God's creature,' says Gerald Wibberley, 'while the part-timer is considered socially to be the lowest of the low.' Part-timing will become much more important, says Wibberley; but there will have to be a change in attitude.

Dr Ruth Gasson of Wye College puts the number of farm households which receive more than half their incomes away from the farm at between 40 and 60 per cent. And the number is rising. According to Gasson part-time farming could help the

103

survival of the family farm, boost the number of new entrants into farming and help stop the decay of rural communities.

In a 1983 report entitled *Gainful Occupation of Farm Families*, Gasson highlights the poor incomes of the small farmers. She carried out a survey of 427 small farms (average 80 acres) in England and Wales. Over 28 per cent of the full-time small farmers earned less than £1000 a year; 48 per cent made between £1000 and £5000; and less than a quarter of the farmers made more than £5000. The most important reason given by the farmers for continuing was living in the countryside, followed by being able to do enjoyable work.

Tenants of small farms also tend to face higher rents than those on larger units. And their rents are rising faster. Farms which had their rents reviewed in 1982 experienced an average 30·7 per cent rise. However, tenants of farms over 600 acres experienced an average 25 per cent rise while for those with less than 120 acres it was 42 per cent. Farms between 120 and 600 acres saw rents rise by an average 33·3 per cent. So while average rents rose by £9 to £31 per acre for the medium size farms, they only rose by £6 to £27 per acre for the largest tenants. It has been suggested that smaller tenants don't have the resources to fight rent increases which landlords demand, though *Farmers Weekly* stated candidly that 'Nobody seems able to explain why it is becoming dearer and dearer to think small.'

A recent poll carried out by the National Farmers' Union among its members revealed that most county branches were in favour of a new code of practice which would prevent landlords amalgamating holdings and would encourage them to maintain a stock of starter farms for young entrants into the industry. It also seems that the EEC is on the verge of introducing measures to combat amalgamation.

As we write there is much debate about a package of tenancy reforms. The Agricultural Holdings Bill is based on a joint NFU/CLA initiative and one of its intentions is to encourage landlords to rent out more of their land. In 1891 over 400,000 holdings were rented and a mere 69,000 farmed by owners. Over 85 per cent of agricultural land was rented. By 1974 a mere 80,000 farms were rented and over 129,000 were farmed by owner-occupiers. Just over half the land area was held by owner-occupiers. The number of tenanted farms has continued to plummet and of the tenanted land falling vacant in 1981 only

11 per cent was relet: a further 50,000 acres was lost from the tenancy system.

The decline in tenancies has been a bitter blow to all those wishing to get into farming. And it has been exacerbated by the steady decline in recent years in the numbers of country council small holdings. The county small holdings schemes have been invaluable in helping entrants get their foot on the first rung of the farming ladder but the present government is encouraging the counties to dispense with them. They will, of course, end up being amalgamated to larger privately owned holdings. In 1982 there were 8,161 county council small holdings covering 395,000 acres. During the year 1981/82 there was a reduction of 3 per cent in the number of equipped holdings (those with house and buildings).

The NFU/CLA package of tenancy reforms will bring about two main changes. First, it introduces a new rent formula. Second, it abolishes the three-generation succession for tenants which was provided by the Labour government in the 1976 Agriculture (Miscellaneous Provisions) Act: existing tenancies will not be affected but new tenancies will enjoy life-time security of tenure only.

Most tenants and many landlords believe that the new Act will do little or nothing to halt the decline in tenanted land. Hew Watt has admirably highlighted the problem of high land prices and high rents: 'It is no use expecting our National Farmers' Union or Country Landowners' Association to solve this problem, for how can they recommend fiscal changes that would reduce the asset value of their members' land?' The main object of reforms, says Watt, should be to reduce the value of vacant land more in line with its real capacity for producing food and timber, and this would inevitably reduce rents. Watt has put forward a series of proposals which he believes would help bring down land prices and increase tenancies by altering the present system of Capital Transfer and Capital Gains taxes, which at present works against landowners who let out their land. He also suggests that capital grant aid should not be given to owner-occupiers of more than 500 acres of lowland or 5,000 acres of upland.[1]

In our next chapter we present a package of proposals whose aim will be to increase the number of farm tenancies, to create much greater opportunities for new entrants who have little capital to get on the farming ladder, and to encourage farmers to employ more labour rather than less.

Branching out

The nature of the agricultural support system has led to landowners and farmers thinking of themselves only as food producers. Consequently many have neglected the other activities that could increase their earnings. For some it may involve adding value to farm produce before it leaves the farm gate: turning milk into yoghurt or cheese, for example. For others it might be through providing bed and breakfast for holiday-makers. And for others forestry may be important. As the support systems for agriculture are gradually dismantled, as they inevitably will be, it will be vital that farmers do more to help themselves. Their survival will often depend on their adventurousness and ingenuity. Let us take a brief trip into the Chilterns with Norman Weiss, a man who has never farmed in his life and probably never will.

Weiss is a tall thin man in his forties. 'We started looking at forestry fifteen years ago,' he said as we cruised out of early morning London on the A40. He ran an investment company which held minority shareholdings in small businesses. 'We had very varied interests, even a company which imported sausage skins.' Forestry, with its generous tax concessions, seemed a sound investment. 'Originally we bought planting land in Scotland and Wales. It was ploughed, fertilized, weeded and planted with Sitka spruce. But after a while we came to the conclusion that it wasn't the best way to invest. It was difficult to control our operations from such a distance. It would take a whole day to drive from London to the forest. When we got there it was usually raining. Then it took a whole day to get back, and if you've seen one Sitka spruce, you've seen them all.'

We slipped through the suburban sprawl of Ruislip and Northwood and turned north into the Chilterns. 'We were producing wood for the low end of the market,' said Weiss: 'pulp and cheap construction timber. They are very vulnerable to world fluctuations – the price of pulp is determined by the Scandinavians, the Canadians and the United States. There used to be some returns from thinnings after about fifteen years but there isn't now. The cost of harvesting is more than the pulp is worth. So we then began to look at lowland forests closer to home. From an economic point of view it seemed better to think in terms of tens of acres of lowland woods than hundreds of acres of upland forests.'

Weiss did not have to start from scratch with planting in the lowlands. He managed to buy fine deciduous woodland with mature standing timber for about half the price of Grade 1 agricultural land. 'In Scotland it costs about £1000 an acre to buy the land and establish a plantation,' he said. 'In the south a woodland, usually containing a proportion of mature broadleaved trees, may be bought for around three quarters of this amount. Thinnings, in the first few years, can recoup a significant proportion of the capital outlay.'

An hour from the centre of London we pull up beside a magnificent deciduous woodland dominated by beech and oak with a smattering of sweet chestnut, hornbeam, rowan, birch, larch and spruce. 'Three years ago I went to Oxford and took the MSc course in Forestry and Land Management,' said Weiss as we plunged into the forest, 'and now I shall concentrate on forestry.' The wood had been neglected and a programme has begun to thin out the mature trees, get rid of the poorer ones and make way for natural regeneration. Weiss will never clear fell. 'Our aim is to keep thinning carefully, improving the quality of the trees and letting the forest regenerate naturally.' Mature timber can be taken out every five years.

Pests can be a problem. We stopped to inspect some badly gnawed larch saplings: 'Dormice,' said Weiss. The edible doormouse, a delicacy much prized by the Romans, escaped from a neighbouring park in the 1930s. In this part of the Chilterns it is as much of a pest as the grey squirrel. Fortunately, it has a terrible weakness for apples. Last year four hundred were caught in apple traps.

Weiss believes quality is very important: 'There will always be people ready to buy the best at the top end of the market.' At the moment veneer-quality oak sells for around £8 a hoppus foot, good quality sweet chestnut for between £4 and £5 and beech for about £2 a hoppus foot. (The hoppus foot is the timber trade's measure of volume, roughly equivalent to a cubic foot.) It is no good just leaving the trees and hoping for the best. They must be selected and managed. The difference between a good oak and a bad one is the difference between £8 a hoppus foot and 80p. And a sweet chestnut with shake (the internal stress fractures which are a common problem) has only a fifth of the value of a decent tree.

'The World Bank and various other bodies,' said Weiss over lunch, 'are pouring vast sums of money into the Third World to grow tropical pines and other fast growing species.' The Food and Agriculture Organization argues that demand will outstrip supply in the next century, but even if there is a world shortage there will be a European glut. Third World countries will treat their timber as a cash crop and sell to the west to get hold of strong currencies. That is why Weiss believes it is better to concentrate on growing high-quality native hardwoods rather than trees like Sitka spuce. The economist Paul Cheshire has argued along similar lines. His arguments and research show why it will be well worth the while of farmers with small woodlands to exploit their high-quality timber. Let us look at them.

Cheshire is scathing about the latest argument used to justify more public spending on coniferous forestry expansion: the impending world timber crisis. Forecasts of impending shortfalls don't bear examination, according to Cheshire: 'They are based on assumptions which are, on a charitable assessment, heroic. . . . Whether you put credence in this impending crisis of world timber supplies or not, seems to me to be essentially a matter of your beliefs and temperament. It is not a matter of objective fact.'

The Forestry Commission was set up after the First War to establish commercial forests in Britain. Justification for massive public spending on softwood afforestation has varied to suit time and circumstance. Originally it was strategic: we would need the wood in future wars. We didn't: ships, planes and other armaments of the Second World War were made out of metal. Subsequently forestry has claimed a role as an import-saver, as a rural employer, and as a provider of recreational sites. Despite a most scathing review of state forestry by the Treasury in 1972, governments have continued to pour money into afforestation with softwoods. 'To be blunt,' said Cheshire at a forestry conference in 1980, 'by the rules of the conventional economic game by which resources in our society are allocated, forestry doesn't have a claim.'

If we take figures for England, where most of the broadleaf

forest is situated, we find that of the 620,000 acres owned by the Forestry Commission 83 per cent is coniferous. Of the 1,185,000 acres in private ownership 58 per cent is deciduous high forest or coppice. In addition there are 417,000 acres of what Timber Growers England and Wales Ltd is pleased to call unproductive woodland, some of which will be fine ancient forest. According to the NFU, the amount of woodland on British farms has increased by 218,000 acres since 1973. However this figure should be treated with considerable scepticism, says Nature Conservancy woodland expert, George Peterken: the ambiguities of the annual surveys make the figures meaningless. Much farm woodland is in the form of small deciduous blocks and its potential is very under-realised. At RURAL's first meeting in 1983 the working party on the creation of productive rural employment commented: 'We consider that one of our greatest under-exploited assets are the small woodlands: we looked in vain for examples of landowners who had come together in this area for mutual profit.'

At a 1983 conference of the British Association for the Advancement of Science, Patrick Leonard of the Countryside Commission revealed that only one per cent of farmers and landowners interviewed in a Commission study had enough basic knowledge to manage their woodlands effectively. He called for a broad-leaved woodland strategy, to be organized by the Forestry and Countryside Commissions, which would give farmers advice on woodland management. Such a programme is sorely needed.

Professor Timothy O'Riordan has suggested that there are over 100,000 owners of woods under five acres in Britain. At present there are few incentives for landowners to improve these woodlands and the EEC support mechanisms are most likely to favour, in the lowlands at any rate, the farmer who grubs out his woods and puts the land down to cereals.

It is evident that farmers could make much better use of their small woodlands. Both the Countryside Commission (generally through local authorities) and the Forestry Commission grant aid management and planting schemes. However, most owners of small woodlands are not in the right tax bracket to benefit from forestry-related tax-relief. This is an important point.

'I emphatically do not support private would-be planters of trees coming and asking for public money to safeguard them against the inherent risk in doing it,' declares Paul Cheshire. Yet he does find that there is a case for helping landowners establish and maintain woods which have an amenity and recreational value. Such a policy, he suggests, would tend to 'support more broad-leaved plantings in lowland Britain accessible to people, [with] more support for indigenous species than for foreign species because of the implications for nature conservation and wildlife. . . . If we want to retain this woodland we will have to pay for it and that implies public funds.'

At the moment our woodlands are in serious decline. Broadleaved woods are being chopped down and planted up with fast-growing conifers for the bottom end of the market. And most farmers are doing little to exploit their small woods. Here is a classic example of where cooperation is needed. Two hundred farmers with 5 acres of woodland apiece will do little in isolation. However if they formed a co-op to manage all the woods as though there was one thousand-acre forest, then the woods would not only be maintained but would yield an economic benefit. The message from men like Weiss is: concentrate on the high quality end of the market; and this means the broadleaved trees like oak, beech, cherry and sweet chestnut.

Country jobs

There are many other ways in which farmers can add value to their produce – thus increasing their earnings and possibly the numbers they employ. For example, since Neil Wates took over Bore Place in Kent in 1976 the workforce has been increased from 7 to 22. This increase has come about not so much through increasing farm labour itself as by establishing other activities such as an engineering unit, a farm consultancy, a study centre and a brickworks. All are self-financing. The farm is about to start making its own cheese and this will bump up the workforce yet again.

This brings us back to the point made by the Country Landowners' Association: it will be the provision of jobs outside agriculture that saves rural communities from total collapse. While we need a shift in agricultural policy to halt the shedding of labour from our farms, it will be the establishment of small industries that will be the salvation of many areas now in decline. Without an injection of industrial jobs, services will continue to decline, villages will continue to get more top heavy, with the old dominating and only the odd sultry youth patrolling the street corners, and those without private transport will become increasingly isolated. Much has already been achieved by the Council for Small Industries in Rural Areas (CoSIRA), an agency of the Development Commission. CoSIRA grant-aids modest schemes to establish small industries, particularly in upland areas. There is one scheme which grant-aids farmers who wish to convert buildings into workshops, small industrial units and so forth. This scheme, which is 35 per cent grant-aided, operates in those parts of England and Wales which are suffering the most serious declines: in most of Cornwall, Devon, Powys, Gwynedd, Dyfed, Lincolnshire, the Peak District, North Yorkshire, Cumbria, Lancashire, Durham and Northumberland. However the amount of money available is very small, especially when compared to the massive sum devoted to sustaining agriculture in less favoured areas.

There is no need to turn the uplands into a vast museum. But if we are not to do so we must pump more money into the creation of small industries. This will mean that we will need not only a relaxation of some planning controls but a more enlightened approach to part-time farming. A valley full of dozens of part-time farmers who have other jobs which fit in with the busy farming periods – hay-timing, lambing and so forth – is infinitely preferable to a valley with only a small number of full-timers.

In 1899 an eccentric Russian suggested that the British countryside needed that special combination of 'Fields, Factories and Workshops'. Peter Kropotkin was a century ahead of his time. What a pity it has taken us so long to realise that. But it's not too late to put the rescue plan into action.

9 De-escalating

'Today no farmer has the choice of farming his land anything
other than intensively. Fixed costs over which he has little or no
control determine that, and this is especially true for the money-
borrower and the rent-payer.' This was the view expressed in
Farmers Weekly in 1983 by Henry Fell, a former vice-chairman
of the Tenant Farmers' Association (a group founded to protect
tenants' rights), and the farmer of 1,800 acres in South
Humberside. Fell went on to suggest that the private landowner
was being progressively usurped by the recently purchasing
owner-occupier – 'heavily mortgaged and over-borrowed,
hoping and praying for high inflation so that today's
extravagance may become tomorrow's bargain' – and the new
institutions, the pension and investment companies. These two
classes manage their land, says Fell, in ways that are both
exploitative and inflationary.

Two weeks later Oliver Walston wrote a piece in the same
magazine speculating on what would happen to him if he shifted
his 3,000-acre farm onto a low-input/low-output system. He
painted a grim picture: if he was selling his wheat at the world
market price of £70 a tonne, rather than the UK price of £120,
he would have the choice of shifting to the low-input system as
practised in the USA or of increasing his inputs. Were he to
decrease them, he claimed, he would have to lower his standard
of living drastically, sack six of his twelve employees, exchange
his office for the tractor seat, plough up rough grazing land and
rip out hedges, and tolerate corn fields full of weeds and
poppies. But, argued Walston, there would be nothing he could
do about the fixed costs. He concludes by saying, 'the more the
price of wheat falls, the more I shall have to try and squeeze
those extra few hundredweight from the land. This will, of
course, mean that I shall probably have to increase my inputs
and not reduce them. I shall have to ensure that, regardless of
what they do in Kansas, I produce more wheat rather than less.'

In view of virtually everything we have said so far, Walston appears to be courting disaster. He is saying that he will be forced to increase output, and thus raise surpluses, and increase inputs, and thus use more support energy.

Dr Mike Wilkinson, the director of RURAL, replied to Walston's piece the following week. Walston's response, according to Wilkinson, was 'predictable but unacceptable'. We must now see why.

Henry Fell highlighted one of British agriculture's most pressing problems, and it is undoubtedly true that the owner-occupier and the farmer who isn't over-borrowed will have lower fixed costs and thus be in a better position to farm in a low-input way. In September 1983 agricultural indebtedness stood at over £4600 million in this country and 25 per cent of farmers' incomes went during the previous year on repaying interest on loans. Some agricultural economists have argued that the industry is not over-borrowed but they tend to base this conclusion on a calculation of borrowing as a percentage of total assets. With land prices ludicrously high this figure is quite modest; if land prices were related simply to the value of the food the land produces, then the calculation would show how seriously in debt the industry really is. Walston, too, is legitimately worried about high fixed costs, but his response shows that he either doesn't know that many farmers (both owner-occupiers and tenants) are successfully running low-input systems, or he is too bound by the post-war ethos of 'increase your yields from all your fields' to change his ways.

A time for thrift

The farming industry faces its worst crisis since the Second World War. By the end of the marvellous summer of 1983 the Community was heading for bankruptcy and a hotch-potch of policies was being mooted in a desperate attempt to save the Community money. Every measure which threatened to diminish in any way the returns to farmers in this country was being met with howls of anguish by the National Farmers' Union and the Milk Marketing Board. Yet none of the protagonists has been prepared to put forward a package of policies which will take farming into the next century in a state of health and solvency. At best, the debates have been concerned with the next five years' development; at worst, and most typically, with the next financial year's balance sheet.

Ten years ago the National Farmers' Union and the Country Landowners' Association exuded confidence and brushed aside criticisms of themselves and their industry with the assurance of lobbies who believe they have the parliamentary decision-makers firmly within their sway. That is no longer the case. The battle against expansionist agribusiness – fought by economists, environmentalists and welfare groups and by many farmers – is slowly being won. Public sympathy for the big farmer has waned and with it the support of Members of Parliament. The Labour and Liberal Parties, as we saw, have pledged themselves to introducing planning controls over agricultural operations, and Tory backbenchers are beginning to accept the critical prognosis of leading economists like J.K. Bowers and Paul Cheshire. Indeed, one of the industry's most powerful and perceptive critics has been Richard Body, Conservative MP for Holland and Boston and author of *Agriculture: The Triumph and the Shame*. One of the more remarkable features of the debate on agricultural spending, on factory farming and on conservation has been the reluctance of the NFU and other leaders in the farming community even to enter it. Criticisms have been countered either by outraged dismissals (not arguments) or by what the NFU and CLA appear to consider their most deadly weapon: silence. Silence is a poor substitute for policy; and in any case it is a weapon to be used sparingly.

Many of the policies which have led to the present plight of the farming industry were conceived in isolation and introduced without any real consideration of their effects on farming as a whole. There is a very real danger that the cures for the present ills will be equally *ad hoc* and will lead to further problems. We must take a more holistic approach but this can only happen if the leaders of the farming community come out of their bunkers and genuinely attempt to sketch out the sort of agriculture we shall have in half a century's time. They must formulate policies that will lead towards it, policies that recognise the impending energy shortages, the restraints on inputs and the inevitable trends towards a healthier diet.

In *Working the Land* we have shown that there are many farmers who are farming in a sustainable and responsible way. There are tens of thousands of others who would like to, but who have been caught on the expansionist treadmill and are not sure how to come off; in short, how to de-escalate.

Our ten-year programme of de-escalation has the following aims: to reduce public spending on agriculture; to get the farm animal out of the factory and back onto the farm; to encourage the mixed farmer and the low-input farmer; to enhance rather than destroy the wildlife and natural beauty of the countryside; to produce food that is not only humanely reared but integral to a healthy national diet; and to ensure that the small farmer and the part-timer do not lose out at the expense of the highly capitalised big farmer. There is one assumption we make, and perhaps it is an optimistic one: that the farming community will put its own house in order fast enough to avoid draconian legislation.

The economic objective

The economic objective is very simple: to reduce public support while at the same time protecting British farmers from depression. It is imperative that financial aid is geared towards helping those who need it to survive, rather than to swelling the bank balances of those landowners who have already become wealthy through public subsidization.

After the House of Lords Select Committee on the European Communities looked at the 1982-83 Farm Price Settlement it produced a scathing report on the Commission's inability to curb excess production. The Committee concluded that a fundamental aim of policy should be to dispose of all excess production competitively on the world market free of all subsidies. We suggest that all such subsidies be phased out over a period of five years. At present it would be unrealistic to imagine that our farmers could compete on the world market with many products and they need to be protected by a system of import levies. But there is absolutely no reason why the public should pay the farmer to produce more than the market requires. Supply must match demand.

Moving mountains

The Keeble Plan, which we discussed in detail in Chapter 6, should become the catalyst to rejuvenate the ailing uplands and encourage the dangerously over-specialised arable producers of the lowlands to revert to a more sustainable form of mixed farming. An immediate start should be made to put it into practice. The following measures must be taken:

* Over ten years the dairy industry must phase out production of calves for beef fattening at the rate of 10 per cent per year. Preferential treatment should be given to dairy producers with herds of under fifty cows. After ten years we shall see nearly all our beef being produced in upland suckler herds.

* At present just over £4 million is spent on grant-aiding cooperatives. This money is administered by Food from Britain. In order to get the Keeble Plan off the ground cooperative ventures to bring the upland and lowland farmers together are vital. Such is the importance of the plan to British farming that we suggest an annual sum of £25 million should be ear-marked for the development and establishment of such cooperatives over the next five years. This figure would also include inducements to get lowland farmers to switch some of their land out of cereals into a venture which, in the transition period and for the immediate future, will prove less profitable. However, with the five-year phasing out of all export subsidies it will be to the advantage of the cereal man to revert to mixed systems. The £25 million should be administered by the County Agricultural Committees (see below) on whom much of the responsibility for reforming agriculture will fall.

Towards mixed farming and sustainability

Obviously the Keeble Plan can only work in those areas where lowlands abut uplands. It would be ridiculous to expect such cooperative ventures to take hold of the extremities of East Anglia. However, we believe the following reforms will help to encourage the low-input and mixed farmer. They represent a broad spectrum of objectives which embrace animal welfare considerations and the need to reduce surplus production.

* The dairy herd should be cut by 25 per cent over the next ten years. It will be up to the Milk Marketing Board and producers to determine how the cuts should be made. At the same time producers should be encouraged to produce low-fat milk and the consumer subsidy on butter must be abolished. We suggest that whatever penalties are introduced to cut

production should be aimed at hitting the producers who rely heavily on concentrate feeding.

* Unfortunately, only legislation can help to better the lot of intensively farmed animals. We suggest the following measures: veal crates should be banned within a year; battery cages within five years; sow stalls and tie stalls within five years. There must also be a ban on live exports of all farm animals and a ban on ritual slaughter. These should be immediate. There should be no ban on veal production but veal should be reared under the loose-house system and animals should be given solid feed after two weeks.

* The use of growth-promoting hormones should be phased out over a five-year period. Farmers will thus be encouraged to leave their animals entire.

* Straw burning must be banned. We suggest that farmers are given a three-year period before the ban becomes law. Many would argue that this is too generous. It does, however, have the merit of giving the arable man time to devise ways of disposing of his straw – for example, through incorporation or use as stock bedding or feed if he decides to move towards mixed farming. The problems of straw disposal will diminish in any case as mixed farming again takes hold in areas which have become predominantly arable.

* British farmers have become dangerously reliant on a massive numbers of chemicals which are used to combat pests and diseases. Many biological farmers show that good husbandry is a far better means of pest and disease control. Organo-chlorine pesticides should be banned immediately. Farmers should be encouraged to minimise their use of chemical controls and ADAS must be given a strong remit to help and encourage farmers to come off the chemical treadmill.

Marketing and labelling

It is vital that the British people know what they eat and how it is produced. For that reason we believe labelling to be of great importance. The manufacturers and retailers of food should have the following statutory duties:

* For all processed meats the percentage content of fat must be given. With unprocessed meat the buyer can assess for him or herself what the fat content is. All meats which come from

animals that have been treated with growth-promoting hormones must be labelled to indicate the fact. (Once hormones have been phased out this will obviously no longer be necessary.) All meat must be labelled to show its area of origin, its breed (in the case of beef) and method of rearing. For example this may read: 'Northumbrian Cheviots – Limousin x Shorthorn – suckler herd'; or alternatively 'Milton Keynes – Hereford x Fresian – barley beef'. Given such a choice it is not hard to imagine what sort of beef production the public will favour in the future.

* Dairy products should always be labelled to show their fat content.
* Processed foods should be labelled to show their percentage content of fat, sugar, salt and so forth.
* We also believe that there should be a system of 'humane labelling for meat'. This will be particularly important during the first five years of the de-escalation plan when battery cages, sow stalls and veal crates are being phased out. The Farm Animal Welfare Committee Executive (FAWCE), a body set up by MAFF, is well placed to define the methods of production that will allow meat to carry the Humane Label.

We suggest that the industry should be given a maximum of two years to switch to this system of honest labelling. Farmers producing vegetables and stock without the use of fertilizers and pesticides often sell through co-ops or shops which indicate the food's origin. Such a practice will undoubtedly continue and become more widespread as more and more farmers come off the chemical treadmill.

It is of great importance that the public should be given more information about the relationship between diet and health. The Department of Health and Social Security should immediately put into effect an educational campaign which will bring to everybody's notice the recommendations of the James Report. One hopes that the British Medical Association will lobby for such a programme in the future.

Future research

At present agricultural research is geared towards high-input/high-output farming. The amount of research into low-input and biological farming is derisory. We believe that a minimum of 10 per cent of the Agricultural Research Council's budget, which is about £70 million, should be given to non-governmental organizations and institutions to carry out such research. Ideal recipients would be organizations like the International Institute of Biological Husbandry and the universities.

Conservation and access

Conservation is nothing more than the wise management of the land. That it can be integrated with profitable farming has been proved by many farmers. It is a matter of great importance to the tax-payer that the British countryside suffers no further destruction through thoughtless and insensitive farming. However, we reject the suggestion that more and more land should be protected through designations and we do not believe that local authority planning controls would prove beneficial to the countryside or acceptable to the farming community. We believe that the ideal vehicle for helping farmers to protect their wildlife and landscape will be the newly constituted County Agricultural Committees. It is appropriate to sketch out their functions here before looking at how they will affect rural conservation.

Professor Gerald Wibberley is among those experts who believe that county committees should be established. He himself was a member of one of the County War Agricultural Committees which so successfully directed farming expansion between 1939 and 1945. The War Committees had considerable power and could evict farmers who were failing to produce the much-needed food. Wibberley was responsible for getting much of the chalk grassland of the South Downs ploughed up and put down to cereals. The Committees continued to operate for some time after the war but gradually their powers were transferred to central government agencies and eventually they were wound up. We now find ourselves with a huge and cumbersome Ministry of Agriculture determining policy with the help of the men in Brussels, and a large centrally run Agricultural Development Advisory Service (ADAS).

'The members of the county committees,' writes Wibberley, 'would be local farmers and landowners, of repute, with other members and advisors from the Countryside Commission, the

Nature Conservancy Council and local planning authorities.' We suggest the following. Each county committee should have a minimum of fifteen members of whom two-thirds should be farmers, landowners and agricultural experts. The remaining third must include representatives from the Nature Conservancy Council, the Countryside Commission, the local planning authority and the regional water authority. Among the two thirds directly involved with farming there should be at least one person who represents the National Farmers' Union, and at least one fifth of the farming section (i.e. two people on a fifteen-person committee) should be tenant farmers. There will, of course, be much debate about the exact constitution of the committees and how their members should be chosen.

These committees will have considerable power and influence. We see the Ministry of Agriculture, and its counterpart north of the border, becoming little more than bankers for the farming world and determinants of overall policy. It will be the committees, each of which will receive an annual budget from central government (much as local authorities do), which will dispense grants and subsidies, determine local policy, ensure that the landscape is conserved and spearhead the de-escalation campaign. Farmers will know that decisions are being made by people who are themselves farmers and who are well respected members of the local community.

Let us return briefly to the business of conservation. We intend to build on the expertise and growing influence of the Farming and Wildlife Advisory Group (FWAG), whose county groups have become expert at drawing up farm maps and working out management plans. The most immediate task, and one which will be vital to the work of the County Agricultural Committees, will involve the drawing up of a New Domesday Book for the British Isles. This should be done by FWAG groups and will be funded by the county committees. It should be quite possible for all the farms in Britain to be mapped over a three-year period. There are huge numbers of naturalists who would be prepared to help voluntarily. Each farm map should carry the following information: percentage of land surface taken up by crops (specified), by temporary grass, permanent grass, water, woodland, scrub, heath and so forth. Features such as copses, hedgerows, streams and archaeological monuments should all be marked with an indication of their age and importance. For example a hedge may be classified as 'ancient species-rich Saxon' or 'post-Second-War hawthorn'. A copy of the map should be lodged with the county committee, with the NCC, with the local authority, with the farmer and, if the farmer is a tenant, with the landowner. On the map those areas which have been considered to be of potential or actual value for wildlife or landscape should be clearly marked and if the farmer wished to alter these he would have to contact the county committee.

For example, the farmer may wish to knock two fields into one. If the hedge on his map is not highlighted as important he can go ahead and grub it out without contacting the committee. However, if it is, he must notify the committee of his intention to grub it out. This can be swiftly done by telephone. At the next committee meeting his intentions will be discussed and he will be told whether or not he can go ahead. The committee may decide that the loss of the hedge would be of no great importance, or it may decide the opposite. If the farmer disagreed with the decision he could take his case to appeal.

Inevitable disagreements will arise among committee members. The NCC representative, although in a minority, will have a power to veto committee decisions which affect conservation. He will, however, use this power sparingly as his life would soon become unbearable if he was seen to act irresponsibly. In cases where the rest of the committee could not accept the veto (and this is only likely to happen when major developments are under scrutiny) the dispute should be referred to a higher level: NCC headquarters and the National Farmers' Union would have to sort out the difference. In the event of their representatives failing to come to a decision, final arbitration would fall to the Secretary of State for the Environment and the Minister of Agriculture. Such a chain of appeals has its precedent in forestry matters today where the NCC is represented on the Forestry Commission's regional committees. The vast majority of disputes are settled amicably.

There may be some farmers and landowners who refuse to go along with the New Domesday Book. That will be their choice but there will have to be a penalty. We suggest that the few intransigents should be ineligible for any form of grant-aid or state help.

The entire system will rely heavily on trust and cooperation and we envisage few serious disputes between either the committees and farmers or between members of the committees. However, despite pleas from the farmers and landowners on the committees there will still be the odd vandal who will be determined to plough up a valuable heath, fell an ancient woodland or drain a rich wetland. He will know that if he tries to go ahead he will make himself ineligible for any financial help in the future and thus it is highly unlikely that he will go against the committee's dictates. If he should still persist with his plans we must have a means of imposing controls. We suggest that the committees should have the power to impose Freeze Orders. These orders would mean that the farmer would be liable to prosecution if he made any attempt whatsoever to alter or change the habitat concerned. It would also mean that he would have no access to the compensation which he might have gained had he accepted the committee's original decision. Furthermore, there would be no question of him negotiating partial development as he might have succeeded in doing had he not decided to go for the jackpot.

Compensation is an important subject. There is a limit to what the nation can afford and the present system of paying farmers an annual sum calculated on loss-of-profits is unacceptable (especially when notional profits include hefty sums of what would have been public money anyway). We believe that the committees should be empowered to give a once-and-for-all payment to farmers who are asked not to develop a particular habitat. However, these payments must be discretionary. Modest sums should be paid to those whose standard of living genuinely suffers through not being able to develop a wet meadow or whatever. Those who are already considered by the committee to be adequately well-off will not receive compensation. Those with healthy bank balances need not bother to apply. It will be up to the farmer to prove his need to the committee.

It almost goes without saying that we believe all grant-aid to farmers and landowners should have conservation criteria built in. Both MacEwen and Sinclair and Potter (see pages 67-9 and 92-6) have suggested perfectly fair and sensible changes to the present Agriculture and Horticulture Grants Scheme and the Agriculture and Horticulture Development Scheme.

We have said little about the subject of access in this book, but that does not imply that it is not important. We envisage access in the lowlands gradually improving with the trend away from intensive arable cultivation towards more extensive stock raising and mixed farming (though we concede that a beef industry based on entire bulls rather than castrated steers will brings its problems). Again, we suggest that access disputes could be ably dealt with by the county committees. The representatives on them from the local authority and the Countryside Commission will be particularly important in determining whether footpaths should be ploughed up, diverted or created.

De-escalation grants

Time and again we talked to farmers who bemoaned their present plight: escalating costs of inputs like fertilizers, sprays and animal feed; high land prices leading to high rents and high insurance payments; dwindling profit margins as yields failed to keep pace with the rising prices of inputs. They all recognised that the present levels of public expenditure on agriculture cannot be maintained for much longer. 'But,' they would say, 'we're trapped. We just can't afford to cut down our inputs.' That is why British farmers will need help over the next ten years; the county committees will help them de-escalate.

There is much that the individual farmer can do to cut down his chemicals bill without any financial inducements. What most need is good advice. Hew Watt wrote in *Farmers Weekly* in 1982 that he was taking on an independent arable adviser on his Essex farm to help guide him off the chemical treadmill. He reported back to the magazine in October 1983. 'We have reduced our spray costs by 30 per cent and our fertilizer by 20 per cent,' he wrote. He had begun to use sprays when problems arose rather than as a blanket insurance policy, and he was saving himself money. 'We also feel we are not playing a part, however small, in encouraging a build-up of resistance in aphids of all kinds by spraying every year.' His last message was full of optimism: 'So to sum up I am no longer just "taking the tablets" of high-input/high-output systems, I am off the treadmill now and, by applying a cost-effective system, have increased my profitability.'

Advice, then, is what a lot of farmers need. Whether or not ADAS, an organization which is so deeply imbued with the old philosophy, is capable of giving such advice remains to be seen. We suggest that specific units within ADAS be set up to give farmers advice solely on the business of coming off the chemical treadmill and reverting to more low-input types of farming.

However, many farmers will need more than advice. They will need some financial help in the form of De-escalation Grants. We are not going to suggest any hard and fast rules for the dispensing of such grants, but we believe they should be discretionary and awarded on the basis of 'to each according to his needs'.

It will be up to the committees and the farming community to decide exactly how the De-escalation Grants should operate. We shall find that farmers will approach the committees and ask for advice about how, for example, to switch from a high-input cereal system to a more benign low-input mixed system. A man with 400 acres down to corn may decide he wishes to pull 100 acres out of corn production and put it down to roots and grass leys so that he can start a rotation which will help him to minimise disease and pests. It may be that he is too far away from the uplands to want to partake in the transhumance programme, but he may decide he needs a flock of sheep or a herd of sows to utilise the 100 acres which have come out of corn production. The committees will be able to help him, or get help for him. He may have no knowledge about sheep and need advice on establishing and running a flock. He may need advice on what root crops to plant, what seed mixes to use for his temporary leys and how to rotate his crops. He may want to have a ten-year programme worked out to de-escalate from his high inputs. Such advice will be provided by the county committees, ADAS or other advisory groups. At the back of his mind he knows that export subsidies are being phased out and support prices squeezed. He will be keen to transform his farm into a mixed enterprise as he knows that having all one's eggs in the same basket is becoming increasingly risky. And he knows that his profit margins for cereals are likely to fall, especially if he continues to rely on heavy inputs. 'But,' he may point out to his county committee, 'if I go into sheep I shall have to erect winter shelter and fences and I just can't afford the capital outlay.' This is where De-escalation Grants come in. They are specifically designed to help farmers switch to systems which are considered beneficial to the country and sustainable. Of course there will be disputes about what sort of enterprises should be favoured, but that is only to be expected. What goes in one area may not go in another. It is impossible to put an exact figure to annual requirements for De-escalation Grants and they will have to be negotiated by the Treasury and the Ministry of Agriculture. One of the aims of this system is to transform the structure of agriculture to ensure that farmers make an adequate living but become much less of a drain on the public purse. We intend to reduce public spending dramatically over ten years. Whatever the cost of de-escalating it will be but a fraction of the present price-support system.

Land and labour

The survival of rural communities will depend as much on investment in non-agricultural activities as on changes in farm policy. However, there is an urgent need to encourage farmers not to shed labour, to encourage landlords to increase the number of available tenancies and to promote part-time farming.

As price support is squeezed and public spending on agriculture reduced, the value of land, in real terms, will fall. We may well find that land prices in ten years time will be roughly the same as they are today. This will mean that they will have been halved in real terms if inflation continues to run at an annual rate of about 5 per cent. Those farmers who have borrowed heavily will find themselves in trouble, though with the fall in land prices we shall see an equivalent fall in rental values. Obviously we do not want to see banks taking over land as their clients are forced to sell to avoid bankruptcy, and we suggest that the county committees should be prepared to help in emergencies by buying land. Farmers who wish to sell part of their land to meet debts would have to give the county committees first option to buy. If the committees decided not to acquire the land on offer, the farmer could then sell on the open market. The price the committee pays for the land would be determined by independent arbitrators (for example, members of the Royal Institute of Chartered Surveyors). Committees would be encouraged to acquire such land on a sale and leaseback arrangement, thus turning the farmer from an owner-occupier into a tenant.

We can thus expect county committees to become large landlords and this will have great advantages. The committees, as landlords, will be able to insist on their tenants adopting farming practices which are considered sustainable, and they will be able to create large numbers of new tenancies. In particular, we expect them to favour small family farms and to hold a large stock of starter farms to help farm workers and others get into farming. We would also like to see the county committees give long-term interest-free or low-interest loans to young people trying to establish themselves as farmers.

We must also encourage landlords to relet tenancies which fall vacant and to create more tenancies. We suggest the following measures:

* No development grants should be available to owner-occupiers with more than 300 acres of lowland, 1,500 acres of marginal land or 3,000 of mountain land.
* All Capital Transfer Tax (CTT) rebates on owner-occupied land should be removed in the case of lowland farms of over 300 acres, marginal farms of 1,500 acres and mountain farms of 3,000 acres.
* CTT rebates on let land should be increased to 50 per cent.
* Capital Gains Tax roll-over relief should apply to owners of let land as well as owner-occupiers.
* Taking let land in hand should be discouraged. We cannot give hard and fast rules but we suggest that whenever a landlord intends to take over a vacant tenancy the county committee must be informed. If the committee believes that the landlord should relet and he refuses to do so, then he should be made ineligible for all forms of state aid. Applications for De-escalation Grants from landlords amalgamating their holdings or taking formerly let land in hand will be viewed extremely unfavourably.

We hope that the county committees will do all in their power to encourage part-time farming, particularly in the uplands. This will mean that they will have to liaise with CoSIRA and the Development Commission to ensure that future non-agricultural developments cater for the working needs of the part-timers. Furthermore, the grant system should no longer discriminate against the part-time farmer.

126

For forty years now agricultural expansion has gone hand in hand with rural decline. The survival of the British countryside and its village communities will depend on more than a reversal of present labour trends on the farm. However a healthy agriculture means a healthy countryside – and a healthy agriculture is one based on people and their skills, not on machines and robots.

Epilogue: *Rural Britain in the Year 2000*

Thirty years of agricultural expansion – which had brought great prosperity to a few farmers, a better standard of living for many, and for the small and marginal farmers continued hardship and often bankruptcy – came to an abrupt halt in the mid-1980s. A disenchanted public, a critical Treasury and a self-destructive farming lobby conspired to bring about an agricultural revolution which imaginative farmers were already presaging and economists and environmentalists were pleading for. While the European Community headed for bankruptcy, largely due to the cost of shifting the massive cereal and dairy surpluses which were themselves the inevitable outcome of the Community's policies, the farming world received its last warning from a plethora of groups and organizations interested in the survival of the British countryside: 'Put your own house in order or we shall do it for you.' The farming press spelt out what this might mean: cumbersome and long-winded applications to local planning authorities every time a farmer wanted to make changes to the landscape of his farm; cuts in public spending which would fall where determined by the 'financial experts' of Whitehall and Brussels rather than by the farming community. . . . It was not a prospect that farmers relished.

Disenchantment grew with the National Farmers' Union and the Country Landowners' Association, as more and more farmers realised that the interests which these two bodies were attempting to protect were those of the big cereal barons and the big dairy producers. With every week that passed what was at first seen as their intransigence was now being construed as stupidity. A combination of enlightened farmers and dissidents within the main farming lobbies recognised that if the farming community was to have any say in the future of the countryside it had to act quickly. And it did.

Two years into the Conservative Party's second term in office farming leaders agreed to the legislation which transferred many of the powers formerly administered by the monolithic Ministry of Agriculture to the reconstituted County Agricultural Committees. A plan to de-escalate British farming was in action by the end of 1987, and the following autumn the first great signs of the transhumance which was to bring prosperity back to the uplands and a saner, better integrated form of mixed farming back to the lowlands signalled the real beginning of the agricultural revolution.

By 1990 factory farming no longer existed. The hen and the pig were back on the land, or at least out of the cage and the tie stall. An increasingly well-informed and health-conscious public demanded better food and got it. The farmer producing lean suckler beef on the hills could get a better price than the man rearing indoors on concentrates. The decline in consumption of dairy products continued throughout the late eighties and early nineties and by the end of the century the dairy herd was barely half of what it was in the crisis year of 1984. With the diminution of the dairy herd more land was freed for extensive rearing of poultry, pigs, beef and sheep and for growing pulses, potatoes and other vegetables whose consumption had increased.

Of course there were some severe problems when the revolution began. Some farmers went hell-for-leather and destroyed valuable wildlife habitats in their quest to make up for what they saw as losses on other farm enterprises. But the county committees proved a highly effective means of self-regulation for the farming community. The great majority of farmers accepted their decisions with good grace. They proved to be fair and sensible in their treatment of the farmers and they handled the awkward task of administering grants and incentives and imposing restraints with a tact which would never have been possible had local authorities been empowered with planning controls as many had envisaged in the early 1980s. The cold war between the Nature Conservancy Council and the farmers – a war which had become increasingly bitter through the 1970s – gradually thawed. Over the years the NCC representatives on the committees acted with commendable fairness and understanding. The main environmental organizations had been sensible enough to invite the NFU and ADAS to give their officers and members a comprehensive training in agricultural practice and economics.

There were, of course, no longer great fortunes to be made in farming. By the beginning of the 1990s farmers were having to dispose of surpluses as best they could on the world market and there were many problems associated with indebtedness. The price of land in 1995 was roughly the same as it was in 1985; in real terms this meant its value had halved. The farmer who had borrowed heavily found himself in trouble with the banks but De-escalation Grants helped many to weather the storm. Where farmers who had over-extended themselves wished to sell a portion of their holdings the county committees established an imaginative scheme to buy their land and set up family farms. County councils, rather than selling off their small holdings as they had once been encouraged to do, were now doing the opposite; and large landlords were given a package of incentives which encouraged them to relet tenancies which fell vacant and to create new ones. The decision that no one should be eligible for development grants if he farmed over 300 acres of lowland, 1,500 acres of marginal land or 3,000 of mountain land led to the break-up of some of the large estates. The part-time farmer, for so long a despised element of the rural community, became increasingly common towards the end of the century. The success of part-time farming, particularly in the uplands, owed much to the shift of small industries into rural towns and villages.

Changes in attitude were even more pronounced than changes in the farming landscape. The process of de-escalation was welcomed by all but a handful of farmers. The sales representatives of the big chemical companies were no longer as welcome as they had been in the halcyon days of the seventies when their produce was slapped on the land with gay abandon. It was with relief that the farmers came off the chemical treadmill: few became strict organic farmers but nearly all relied heavily on their skilful manipulation of rotations and stock to curb pests and disease. There were some long-established traditions, ridiculed in the post-war boom period, that came back into fashion. Interestingly, much of the impetus for change came from the new generation of farm students who had little sympathy for the reckless ways of many of their parents.

Had anybody, twenty years earlier, correctly forecast what

the landscape of the year 2000 would look like, his vision would probably have been dismissed as utopian, impracticable and perhaps even undesirable. To transform British farming so dramatically and so quickly would be impossible, it would have been claimed.

As it turned out it was all remarkably easy. Farmers are marvellous at adapting to change when they believe it is necessary. And they did believe it was necessary. They wanted to survive far into the next century.

Glossary

CAP: The Common Agriculture Policy of the European Community.

Ewe: A female sheep.

FYM: Farmyard manure: a mixture of dung, urine and straw bedding.

Headage payments: Payments made per head of stock, for example by the EEC to hill farmers for sheep.

Insecticide: Chemical used to kill insects.

Nematocide: Chemical used to kill nematode (round) worms.

Slurry: A liquid mix of dung, urine and water.

Steers: Castrated male cattle.

Store cattle: Cattle for fattening.

Suckler cow: A cow whose main purpose is to produce and suckle her calves rather than give milk for human consumption.

Transhumance: The transfer of stock from winter to summer pastures and vice-versa.

Unit: A measure of quantity for fertilizer equal to one hundredth part of a hundredweight (1.12 lb)

Additional Information

1 *The Measure of the Problem*

1 Average wheat yields rose from 4·33 tonnes per hectare to 6·2 tonnes in the decade after we joined the EEC. During the same period the average yields per cow rose from just under 4000 litres a year to just under 5000. An unfortunate cow by the name of Ledmore Julie, an inhabitant of Hampshire, produced a colossal 18,450 litres in 305 days in 1982; that is, around 150 pints per day. Record wheat yields now stand at over 15 tonnes per hectare. Similarly yields have risen for barley, oats, potatoes, sugarbeet and rape.

2 Of the tenanted land falling vacant in 1981 only 11 per cent was relet. Between 1972 and 1982 the number of farm holdings fell by 16·43 per cent in England and rather less in Wales. Combined returns compiled by MAFF showed a 40 per cent decrease in holdings under 2 hectares; a 15 per cent decrease for the 20 to 40 hectare range; a 5 per cent decrease in the 40 to 200 hectare range; and a 13 per cent increase in the numbers of holdings over 200 hectares. These staggering figures are reflected differently between the counties. The most spectacular declines in the number of farms are found in Bedford, Norfolk and Yorkshire (down 24 per cent, 23 per cent and 19 per cent respectively), and the lowest declines were in Dorset and Devon (down 7·3 per cent and 10·7 per cent).

2 *Food Fit for People*

1 The systems of support are extremely complex. For example butter and SMP (skimmed milk powder) are supported by the imposition of levies on milk imports, by payments of refunds on exports, by support buying and by assistance towards the costs of private storage of products. And there are consumer subsidies payable on butter which is to be consumed direct.

3 *Animal Factory*

1 This is good news for the drug companies. Sales of veterinary medicines in the EEC countries for 1981 (excluding Eire, Greece and Luxembourg) reached £567 million. Veterinary bills cost on average about 1 to 1·5 per cent of the cost of raising livestock.

2 As we write, periodic press releases from the National Farmers' Union drop onto the doormat with news of the final stages of the Aujeszky's disease eradication scheme. On 2 August 1983 the NFU release announced that

300,000 pigs from 350 herds had been slaughtered since the beginning of the eradication scheme. 'In general veterinary terms the scheme is progressing well,' announced the release rather cryptically. Total compensation paid out had reached £17,000,000. Exactly a month later came another press release announcing that over 325,000 pigs from 399 herds had been slaughtered. Compensation had reached £19,000,000.

3 In economic terms it is difficult to see the advantages of the crate system. The cost of loose housing works out at around £78 a calf compared with £175 in crates. At the 1982 Smithfield Show 18 of the 33 veal exhibits were from loose houses, the rest from crates. Twelve of the 14 winners came from loose houses.

90 per cent of the veal served in restaurants and hotels in Britain is from Holland. We import 90,000 crated veal carcases a year, many of which crossed the sea from Britain in the first days of their life.

4 For years there has been dispute over the definition of free range. The law has defined the indefinable in a Shropshire court case in 1983. To be free range a bird must have access to the outdoors and obtain a significant proportion of its feed from the land. Maximum stocking density is defined as 150 birds an acre. Among other systems of less intensive egg production are the deep litter housing with outdoor runs stocked at the rate of up to 3,000 birds an acre, the aviary system which is similar to deep litter but makes better vertical use of the building, and the straw yards system where birds are kept in covered yards and on straw. All of these systems allow the birds a degree of movement to fulfil their behavioural patterns.

Paul Carnell of Earth Resources Research Ltd has attempted to compare the economics of the various systems. He has noted that increases in egg yields over the last twenty years have been just as dramatic under free range and deep litter conditions as they have been in batteries. The comparisons are interesting. The number of birds which can be managed by one person are estimated as follows: battery, 10,000; aviary, 9,000; deep litter, 8,000; straw yard, 4,500; free range, 1,800. Estimates of annual egg yield per bird are 260 for battery, 245 for deep litter, 240 for aviary, the same for straw yards and 220 for free range (though the Smiths' hens average 273 eggs a year). Feed consumption, measured in terms of grams for each egg produced is 165 for battery, 174 for deep litter, 179 for aviary, 190 for straw yard and 200 for free range. Carnell's egg production costs work out per dozen at 44p, 48p, 49p, 54p and 67p for the five systems.

5 Meat and Livestock Commission comparisons for 1982 between free rangers and intensive units are not as accurate as one would wish as out of the 17 free range herds being studied four had failed to log variable costs in detail and only four had attempted to log fixed costs. The data available, however, gives us some indication why an increasing number of producers are returning to farrowing sows outdoors.

The culling rate of sows outdoors and the replacement rates were considerably lower than for the entire MLC sample of 766 herds (figures in each case are for outdoors first and the 766 herd sample second): sow mortality 2·7 per cent and 3·5 per cent; culled sows 34·7 per cent and 36·8 per cent; replacements 33·1 per cent and 45·8 per cent). Although outdoor sows produced fewer litters a year than the rest (2·06 compared to 2·21), piglet mortality was lower (0·66 per litter compared to 0·78). Outdoor units weaned later then the rest by an average 6 days (32 days outdoor average). Feed costs worked out to be more outdoors (£11.23 compared to £9.63).

6 The National Union of Agricultural and Allied Workers had this to say in its submission to the Agriculture Committee. 'As to workers' personal preference, the view seems to be that they would prefer to work out of doors, and that is often why they choose to work in agriculture. In the pig industry it is felt that most workers would prefer to look after sows on the extensive so-called Roadnight System, rather than keeping sows permanently in buildings. Poultry workers have also expressed dissatisfaction with the heat and dust that appear always to be present in intensive poultry houses.'

The Union considered the tendency to cram as many creatures into as small a space as possible to be objectionable. Farm workers were said to be disturbed by systems which prevented animals from moving around 'adequately' and they considered the innoculation of hormone pellets by syringe gun cruel. 'Many farm workers appear to find battery cages objectionable. . . . Some members object to the system whereby sows are kept tethered during a large part of pregnancy – this is thought to be cruel.'

It is certainly true that many farmers and farm workers find intensive pig and poultry production repugnant. 'I'd rather work on the roads than have anything to do with an intensive pig unit,' said one farm worker friend on a Yorkshire farm.

4 *Muck and Straw: The Parable of Waste*

1 Since the war the pig business has expanded rapidly on Humberside. In 1960 there were 171,000 pigs in the East Riding. Twenty years later there were over 650,000. Ten per cent of the nation's pigs are domiciled on Humberside, and of them 4 out of every 10 live in the Borough of Holderness. Disposal of waste has been as much a problem as smell.

2 In September 1983 *Farmers Weekly* reported that the problem has now become so serious that livestock farmers may soon be banned from spreading slurry in the winter months. ADAS officials have worked out that this could cost individual farmers up to £20,000 in having to build extra storage space to keep their muck out of water courses through the winter. ADAS figures for 1982 showed that there were 64 convictions for pollution, 17 of them because slurry tanks were overflowing. There were 1,215 written warnings to farmers, a fifth of them prompted by overflowing slurry. There is no doubt that water authorities will get tougher as the problems increase.

3 This low level of manure and slurry application is partly the result of the disintegration of mixed farming, partly a consequence of cheap bag fertilizers encouraging the farmer to ignore the potential value of FYM and slurry and partly because the nutrients in manures are not always in the proportions the

farmer wants for his crops. 'Thus,' say RURAL, 'although the requirements for potash by arable crops and grass may be easily met by application of manures, the adverse effects of an excess supply of potash impose limits on the total quantity of manure which may be applied per hectare of land.' The available nutrients vary according to the type of manure and its origin, as the table taken from MAFF sources below shows:

	N	P	K
Cattle FYM (kg/tonne)	1.5	2.0	4.0
Cattle Slurry (kg/1000l)	1.5	1.0	4.5
Pig Slurry	4.0	2.0	2.7
Poultry Slurry	9.1	5.5	5.4

Cattle manure, which is low in N, can supply all the phosphate and potash but not the high amounts of nitrogen required by the nitrogen-greedy strains of modern grass. Pig slurry, however, is virtually a complete fertilizer for cereal crops, and poultry manure is exceptionally rich.

5 *Coming Off the Chemical Treadmill*

1 ICI is by far the biggest of the 33 companies which are members of the UK Fertilizer Manufacturers' Association, with about 60 per cent of supplies. Norsk Hydro (who bought Fisons) have about 25 per cent of the market and UKF 10 per cent. Unfortunately for the farmers, fertilizer prices, which have remained relatively stable over the last couple of years as a result of a price war between the big manufacturers, will rise steadily as oil becomes scarcer and more expensive.

2 In 1985 the maximum permitted level of nitrates in water in EEC countries will be reduced from 100 parts per million (ppm) to 50 ppm. Britain's water authorities, already straining to control pollution of our lakes and rivers from agricultural waste, domestic sewage and industrial effluent, will have to take action against these high levels. Water authorities have various options. The first is to blend high and low nitrate water together to produce an acceptable mix. This is very costly. The second is to remove nitrates from the water by ion exchange. This, too, is very expensive. The third solution, and the one which makes sense in the long run, is for the water authorities to pass the problem back to the farmer.

3 However, as an article in *Farmers Weekly* pointed out in July 1983, the plough is as much to blame as bag fertilizers. 'On land over the aquifer layers, use of nitrogen fertilizer has dramatically increased in the past 20 years and will have made the nitrate problem worse. But the move from grassland to arable has been even more detrimental.'

Organic matter in permanent pasture can tie up 10 tonnes of nitrogen on a hectare and annual leaching losses from a well established sward are normally less than 10 kg of N, not enough to cause any problems. However ploughing up in the autumn exposes organic matter to the air and nitrates can be leached out in huge quantities. *Farmers Weekly* reported one experiment where 200 kg of nitrogen a hectare were released in the first year after ploughing. It seems that permanent pasture suffers the lowest rate of nitrogen leaching. Worst of all is land down to spring cereals. It is salutory that the good low-input farmer will try to plough as shallow as possible, which will help to counter the problem.

4 Conservative estimates suggest that, worldwide, 10,000 people die from pesticide poisoning each year and a further 375,000 are poisoned though not killed. The British chemical industry does very well out of pesticide exports: in 1978 the UK had over 12 per cent of the world's trade. In 1983 British pesticide sales were worth £540 million, half of which came from exports. When the European Parliament drafted a directive in 1983 which would have banned the sales abroad of restricted pesticides without prior written consent from recipient governments, there was an outcry from the British Agrochemicals Association. The Commission, however, took the point of view of the chemical companies. Britain will continue to sell at least 11 pesticides which are severely restricted on health or environmental grounds under the far from draconian laws of either the EEC or Britain.

5 'If the various pressure groups had succeeded, if there had been a world ban on DDT as many sought, then Rachel Carson and her book *Silent Spring* would now be killing more people in a single year than Hitler killed in the whole holocaust.' This was Dr D.G. Hessayon, the chairman of the British Agrochemicals Association (BAA) from 1980 to 1981. DDT had a dramatic effect in many Third World countries in reducing malaria by killing the Anopholes mosquito. Malarial incidence was reduced from about 75,000,000 cases in India in the early fifties to 49,000 in 1961, an astonishing achievement attributable to the pesticide. But by 1976 the number of cases of malaria had risen to 6,500,000, and each year sees further increases. According to the United Nations Environmental Programme (UNEP) many strains of malarial mosquitoes are now resistant to DDT.

6 *Moving Mountains*

1 The House of Lords Select Committee on the European Communities looked at the 1982-83 Farm Price Settlement and concluded that 'it is now essential that the Commission should come forward with effective proposals for making the thresholds bite, especially those for milk and cereals; it is equally essential thereafter that prices should not be set at levels which would nullify decisions on the thresholds and undermine realistic production objectives. The aim should be that all production in excess of such objectives should be disposed of competitively on the world market free of subsidies.' The Lords are asking the farmer to return to the market place where output must be related to demand. The halcyon days of generous export subsidies and intervention buying are nearly over.

8 *Land, Labour and Accountancy*

1 Capital Transfer Tax was introduced in 1974 as a single tax payable by the donor on the transfer of property. CTT is subject at present to a 50 per cent

Agricultural Relief on land and buildings up to 1000 acres or £250,000 and a 50 per cent Business Relief on assets such as plant and machinery. The 1979 Northfield Report into the Acquisition and Occupancy of Agricultural Land (commissioned by the last Labour government) suggested that CTT encouraged owner-occupancy at the expense of tenancies as landlords are granted low CTT relief and that it has possibly encouraged amalgamation. Consequently Hew Watt suggests that CTT rebates on let land should be increased from 20 per cent to 50 per cent. He also suggests that Capital gains Tax roll-over relief should apply to owners of let land as well as to owner-occupiers.